OFF THE
BEATEN
(SUBWAY)
TRACK

OFF THE BEATEN (SUBWAY) TRACK

NEW YORK CITY'S BEST UNUSUAL ATTRACTIONS

· SUZANNE REISMAN ·

CUMBERLAND HOUSE
NASHVILLE, TENNESSEE

OFF THE BEATEN SUBWAY TRACK
PUBLISHED BY CUMBERLAND HOUSE PUBLISHING, INC.
431 Harding Industrial Drive
Nashville, TN 37211

Cover design: James Duncan Creative
Text design: Lisa Taylor

Library of Congress Cataloging-in-Publication Data

Reisman, Suzanne.
  Off the beaten (subway) track : New York City's best unusual attractions / Suzanne Reisman.
     p. cm.
  ISBN-13: 978-1-58182-641-8 (pbk.)
  ISBN-10: 1-58182-641-9 (pbk.)
  1. New York (N.Y.)—Guidebooks. 2. Curiosities and wonders—New York (State)—New York—Guidebooks. 3. Subways—New York (State)—New York—Guidebooks. I. Title. II. Title: Off the beaten track.

  F128.18.R45 2008
  917.47'10444—dc22

                                                                          2008018759

Printed in Canada
1 2 3 4 5 6 7 — 14 13 12 11 10 09 08

To Justin, my favorite unusual attraction

CONTENTS

Acknowledgments - 11

Introduction - 13

LOWER MANHATTAN (BELOW 14TH STREET)

Skyscraper Museum - 21

Fraunces Tavern Museum - 25
  archeological dig sites - 28

New York City Police Museum - 29

American Numismatic Society/
New York Federal Reserve Bank - 32
  Little Lad's Basket - 34

Museum of American Finance - 35
  Jeremy's Ale House - 36

Lower East Side Troll Museum - 37
  Pickle Guys - 40
  Economy Candy - 40
  Yonah Schimmel's Knishery - 40

New York City Fire Museum - 41
  Rice to Riches - 43

Dia Center for the Arts: "The New York
Earth Room" and "The Broken
Kilometer" - 44

Museum of Comic and Cartoon Art - 46

Ukrainian Museum - 48
  Galeria De La Vega - 50
  Obscura Antiques - 50

Forbes Galleries - 51
  *14th Street A,C, E Subway
  Station - 56*

MIDDLE MANHATTAN (14TH STREET TO 59TH STREET)

Theodore Roosevelt's Birthplace - 59
  Eisenberg's Sandwich Shop - 61

Masonic Hall and Chancellor Robert R.
Livingston Masonic Library and
Museum of Grand Lodge - 62

Chapel of Sacred Mirrors - 67

Horticultural Society of New York - 69

United Nations Sculpture Garden - 70
  Waterfall Walkway - 71
  Berlin Wall - 71

Tourneau Gallery of Time and Oris
Exhibit Hall - 72

UPPER MANHATTAN EAST (ABOVE 59TH STREET, EAST OF 5TH AVENUE)

Corning Gallery at Steuben Glass - 75

Mt. Vernon Hotel Museum & Garden - 76
  Tender Buttons - 79

Museum of American Illustration - 80

Herbert & Eileen Bernard Museum of Judaica at Temple Emanu-El - 83

New York Academy of Medicine Library - 86

Museum of the City of New York - 88
   Charles A. Dana Discovery Center - 90

National Museum of Catholic Art & History/Our Lady of Mt. Carmel Church - 91

UPPER MANHATTAN WEST (ABOVE 59TH STREET, WEST OF 5TH AVENUE)

Ertegun Jazz Hall of Fame - 97

Nicholas Roerich Museum - 98

Cathedral of St. John the Divine - 101
   Hungarian Pastry Shop - 107
   Harlem Market/Malcolm Shabazz Mosque - 107
   Amy Ruth's - 107

Trinity Cemetery and Mausoleum - 108

Museum of Art and Origins - 110
   Jumel Terrace Books - 112

National Track & Field Hall of Fame - 113
   Mini George Washington Bridge Playground - 115
   El Malecón - 116
   Highway Living - 116
   Site of Fort Washington - 116

St. Frances Cabrini Shrine - 117

Dyckman Farmhouse Museum - 121
   Scavengers of Inwood - 123

Inwood Hill Park - 124
   Albert's Mofongo House - 126

THE BRONX

Judaica Museum of the Hebrew Home for the Aged - 129
   Loeser's Kosher Delicatessen - 131

Edgar Allan Poe Cottage - 132
   Original Products - 135
   258th Field Artillery Armory - 135

Hall of Fame for Great Americans - 136
   Aqueduct Walk - 138

Our Lady of Lourdes Grotto at St. Lucy's Church (a.k.a. Lourdes of America) - 139

Maritime Industry Museum at SUNY Maritime College - 142

QUEENS

Steinway & Sons Piano Factory Tour - 149
   Astoria bakeries and food mini-tour - 152

Socrates Sculpture Park - 153
   Bohemian Hall and Beer Garden - 155

5 Pointz - 156

Louis Armstrong House - 158
   El Indio Amazonico - 164

Queens Museum of Art - 165

Poppenhusen Institute - 169

The Living Museum at Creedmoor
Psychiatric Center - 172

Queens County Farm Museum - 176

BROOKLYN

City Reliquary - 183

Shrine Church of Our Lady of Mt.
Carmel - 187

Brooklyn Brewery Tour - 189
SKSK - 191

New York City Transit Museum - 192

Prison Ship Martyrs Monument - 194

Waterfront Museum - 196
Brooklyn Superhero Supply Co. - 199
Steve's Authentic Key Lime Pies - 199

Weeksville Heritage Center - 200

Floyd Bennett Field - 204

Enrico Caruso Museum of America - 207

Coney Island Museum - 211
*Nathan's Famous and the Hot Dog
Eating Wall of Fame* - 216

Harbor Defense Museum - 217
John Paul Jones Park - 220

STATEN ISLAND

Staten Island Museum - 223
*Professional Baseball Scouting Hall
of Fame* - 225
Our Lady of Mt. Carmel Shrine - 226
Garibaldi Meucci Museum - 229
*Castleton Hill Moravian Church
Labyrinth Walk* - 232
Noble Maritime Collection - 233

Index by Category - 237

ACKNOWLEDGMENTS

Many thanks to my "helper monkeys" (Stephanie Adams, Roger Chi, Paula Denoya, Sara Marks, Desiree Miltimore, Jenny Occhipinti, Justin Pollack, Scott Pollack, Rachel Samlan, Oliver Swan, and Stef Weiss) for sharing so many adventures with me; my friend and agent Matthew Elblonk for helping me share my adventures in book form; and my family for their love and support through years of "adventures." I could not have done it without you.

INTRODUCTION

I love road trips, strange museums, and eccentric people who share their unusual talents, passions, and obsessions with the general public. While I happily reside in Manhattan, I jealously spent years reading about interesting historic sites, crazy monuments, nostalgic diners, and buildings designed to resemble something else—e.g., a building in the shape of a giant duck or a pharmacy shaped like a mortar and pestle—around the United States. (Perhaps my interest in these things was honed at a young age; when I was a tot growing up in the suburbs of Chicago, I received my first swimming lessons at a YMCA that resembled the Leaning Tower of Pisa.) If New York City is the largest, most diverse city in the country, why was it so hard for me to find unusual sites to see and things to do that didn't require long drives? Sure, I understand that New Yorkers face real estate constraints unheard of anywhere else in the country, but I figured there *must* be interesting places within the five boroughs that adventure seekers like me could get to with the subway and/or bus.

I believe that New York is the best city on earth. During my ten-year career in community development, I spent time in a variety of communities across the City that will never get attention from travel magazines but which offer tremendous opportunities to see and do new things, not to mention feast like royalty. Taking advantage of our public transportation led me to discover that there are oodles of interesting things to see and do in the City that give any roadside attraction a run for its gas money. It turns out that the ultimate road trip is the one taken on the subway tracks.

Don't get me wrong; I love a good road trip as much as anyone. But road trips are special occasions usually requiring several days off from work, and most people who live in New York City don't own an automobile. Why not save some money and shrink your carbon footprint by taking a "road trip" using New York's fine public transportation to visit something different? This book explores unusual attractions that are off the beaten (subway) track that easily match anything for which you would need a car to see. With almost 850 miles of subway track, over twenty-five subway lines (including three shuttles), and 486 stations in New York City, where *can't* you go? You can travel thirty-eight miles with only one transfer. There are also more than 200 bus routes covering hundreds—if not thousands—of miles of urban territory. Mass transit can carry an adventurous soul to many unusual attractions within the City, often away from the hustle and bustle of stressed New Yorkers and the usual, crowded tourist areas.

Think about it: New York has the more densely populated blocks in the country, yet a single subway ride from Times Square will leave you utterly alone, surrounded by (mostly) silent nature in the woods of Inwood Park. There are skyscrapers galore in Manhattan, but the subway and bus can bring you to a working farm in Queens. In a city where millions of dollars are spent acquiring fine art, there is a psychiatric hospital with a working gallery of its residents' artwork that is open to the public by appointment. You can join the hoity-toity at the Metropolitan Opera House, or you can listen to turn-of-the-century recordings of opera legend Enrico Caruso played on vintage phonographs in a museum on the second floor of a two-family home in Brooklyn. The body of a venerated saint, shrines that heal the ailing, and religious relics are located not very far from enormous balls of hair coughed up by cows. New York City is loaded with enough offbeat attractions to keep a curiosity seeker busy for quite some time, no car required.

Off the Beaten (Subway) Track is designed to help people find the unusual and quirky sites in New York City that even many lifelong New Yorkers don't know about. This book is for New Yorkers and visitors who want to avoid Times Square and see more of the "real" city. It is organized by geographic regions to encourage the exploration of the cultures and variety of New York City's many great neighborhoods while making your way to the destination of your choice.

An upfront admission: Since the book is a labor of love, it is heavily influenced by my personal preferences and interests. I especially like bakeries, Southern cooking, Jewish heritage, Catholic shrines, and historic sites of somewhat limited importance. (A Bronx cottage containing the bed that Edgar Allan Poe's wife died in? I am *so* there!) Oddities and grotesqueness delight me, but I also enjoy normal places that have some hidden treasures. Gift shops also figure prominently into my preferences, as half the time they are as much fun to browse as the museum or attraction for which they raise money to support. Interesting neighborhood shopping and eating opportunities are highlighted in this book as well. There's no rhyme or reason why many of the places are included in the book; I just happen to like them.

As many of these sites depend on one person to operate, be sure to call before you set out for your destination. Checking official websites is a good start, but that is not always enough as the information may not be updated. Small museums and other interesting attractions frequently change hours of operation, sometimes change locations, and often are under-staffed. If a special event is taking place, the attraction may be closed even if it usually is open at the time you plan to visit. Countless times, I foolishly did not follow my own advice and found myself standing grumpily on the stoop of some closed building in the outer reaches of a borough after I spent ninety minutes getting there via bus and subway. Half the fun may be getting there, but still, don't let this happen to you—call beforehand.

Further, it is critical to consider the effects of rapid gentri-fication. The history of New York City *is* constant change. I learned from my community development experience that there are almost no sites in the City that haven't been some-thing else in a previous life or two. From the time I began research for this book two years ago to when I finished it, many unique sites have closed. One day I was eating a hamen-tashen in front of a Lower East Side bakery, the next day the bakery was a hole in the ground, being prepared for its new use as yet another glass and steel luxury condominium. (Rest in peace Gertel's Bakery Since 1915, the Caribbean Costume Museum, the African-American Wax Museum of Harlem, and the Museum of the Mikveh. I hardly knew ye.) Again, calling ahead to make sure the site you want to visit still exists is a solid plan.

After verifying if and when you can indeed visit a place, the next step to a successful subway road trip is to figure out how to get there. Some places have websites with excellent directions; others don't even have phones. Fortunately, there are several great trip planning resources on the Internet, each with benefits and drawbacks.

GOOGLE MAPS	NYPIRG'S STRAPHANGERS CAMPAIGN	ON NY TURF	HOP STOP	
• After entering destination address, provides a map of immediate area, indicating the locations of the nearest subway stops • Map includes a wide range of the surrounding streets • Can re-center or zoom in and zoom out of map for different views of vicinity • Can pull up a satellite image overlay for more details • For those walking to a destination, door-to-door directions are available, with distance estimate	• After entering destination address, provides a map of immediate area, indicating the location of the nearest subway stops • Can re-center or zoom in and out of map for different views of vicinity • Links to MTA website so you can check for scheduled service changes due to repairs	• After entering destination address, provides a map of immediate area, indicating the locations of the nearest subway stops • Using Google map technology, can produce a hybrid subway map with satellite overlay • Includes PATH train for those coming from northern New Jersey	• After entering starting address and destination address, provides detailed door-to-door directions, including subways, buses, regional rail, and walking options • Accounts for subway repairs and service changes in suggested routes • Includes a list of every subway and/or bus stop along the route so you can anticipate when to get off and how long it will take to get there • Can request alternate suggestions	P R O S

GOOGLE MAPS	NYPIRG'S STRAPHANGERS CAMPAIGN	ON NY TURF	HOP STOP
• No information about bus service is provided • Door-to-door directions are for driving, so they are not always the most direct path and they estimate travel times by car, not walking	• Map has very narrow range • No door-to-door directions for walkers • No information about bus service is provided	• No door-to-door directions for walkers • No information about bus service is provided	• Accompanying maps are useless • Routes are not always the most convenient way to go • In certain cases, the suggested route was not accurate

C O N S

If, even after all the mapping and planning, you are lost, just ask someone for help. When I first moved to New York, non–New Yorkers advised me to never look lost; never take out a map; and never, ever, under any circumstances, stop someone on the street for directions or else be mugged/beaten/killed. This could not be further from the truth. As a friend reminded me, we New Yorkers love to show off how much we know about our hometown. People are almost always willing to give directions or show you the way, provided you do not inconvenience them too much. For example, my friend Nancy and my sister once visited me from Chicago. When they got lost on their way to South Street Seaport, a man with a black trench coat stopped and offered to help them. "You want directions?" the guy asked. He suddenly yanked his trench coat open. They gasped, expecting to be flashed. The fully clothed man instead revealed pockets stuffed with maps. He daintily pulled one out, showed them where they currently were, highlighted their route, and off he went on his merry way.

Now it's your turn. Load up your MetroCard and explore the City on a subway road trip of your own!

LOWER

·

MANHATTAN

SKYSCRAPER MUSEUM

Address: 39 Battery Place

Phone: 212.968.1961

Directions: 4 or 5 to Bowling Green; 1 to Rector Street;
    R or W to Rector Street

Other details at: www.SkyScraper.org

For such a tall subject, the Skyscraper Museum is surprisingly small. It offers one traveling and one permanent exhibit in a sleek space at the back of a Ritz Carlton hotel. The shiny metal floors and mirrors on the ceiling reflect the exhibit materials nicely.

After paying my admission in the mod gift shop, I found myself traveling back to a quainter time as I walked up the ramp to the exhibits. Two walls are made of green, frosted glass and display old black-and-white photographs of the construction of skyscrapers and other large buildings in New York City.

After studying pictures of stoic men sitting on squat steel beams eating sandwiches from lunch pails, I was propelled into the twenty-first century by the temporary exhibit on the Burj Dubai, which is projected to be the world's tallest building when it is completed. (Its ultimate altitude is a secret while the building is under construction so that no one else can throw a spire onto the top of their existing building and outdo them before construction is even complete on the tower.) While reading the sordid details of the project (for example, 3,000 to 6,800 laborers toil on the Burj Dubai daily) and learning about Dubai's growth (over 350 thirty-story or higher buildings are currently under construction), I decided that this exhibit could just as accurately be titled Human Hubris.

The exhibit also includes interesting information on skyscrapers in general. A timeline with drawings and general height information documents the tallest buildings and structures built since 1890. On a global map of super-tall buildings, two-dimensional buildings jut from the earth at a scale of 1:2400 to illustrate where the tallest buildings are clustered. Asia dwarfs the entire western hemisphere in sheer numbers. All of the older skyscrapers are in the United States, and the newer ones are in Europe and Asia.

Buried in all this—something I always wondered—is an explanation of what constitutes a skyscraper and how buildings are measured. A skyscraper is by definition occupiable; structures, on the other hand, are not for occupancy. The Council on Tall Buildings and Urban Habitat lays out four ways in which to measure skyscrapers and structures: to the structural top; to the highest occupied floor; to the top of the roof; and to the tip of the spire or antenna. All measurements begin at pavement level from the main entrance.

The significance of the four different ways to measure the height of a skyscraper plays out in the Skyscraper Museum's permanent exhibit, Twentieth Century Towers.

A display dedicated to the Sears Tower in Chicago, which was the tallest building in the world until the Petronas Towers were built in Malaysia in 1998, explains its design. More important in my opinion, it also shows how Petronas Towers stole its title by cheating. Drawings comparing the two buildings measures Petronas's height to its pinnacle, but the Sears Tower's height is measured to the roof; the difference is thirty-three feet. If the antenna on the Sears Tower were included in the measurements, it would far exceed the height of Petronas Towers. Let's set the record straight here: Chicago still rules! (As a former Chicagoan, this is important to clarify.)

The rest of the Skyscraper Museum focuses on New York City. There's a survey of building technology in the City, but the bulk of the exhibit is devoted to specific buildings of note. Through old photo souvenirs, illustrated books, postcards, plans, and diagrams, I gleaned much information about the Woolworth Building, the Empire State Building, 14 Wall Street Bankers Trust, the 1894 American Surety Building (the first in New York City built using an all-steel frame), 48 Wall Street Bank of New York, and 1 Chase Plaza. Yet the addresses for many of the buildings are not part of the displays, so it is hard to say where some of them are located if you later want to visit them yourself. Another display case is full of undated illustrated postcards depicting assorted buildings throughout New York. (My favorite one is signed, "November 14, 1905, With Love, May.")

No museum dedicated to skyscrapers or New York

City is complete without something on the World Trade Center. The Skyscraper Museum offers photos and a model of the Twin Towers. A panoramic picture reminded me just how striking they were, hovering over all the other tall buildings in the Financial District. Details about the buildings' design are presented and a video documenting the construction process plays on loop. The exhibit ends with a small display on the gauche Freedom Tower to be built on the Trade Center site.

The museum's gift shop sells books about New York and skyscrapers, models of famous buildings, postcards, and other assorted junk. Look for the postcards from which you can build teeny, paper scale models of skyscrapers, mostly of Chicago's architectural and engineering triumphs.

FRAUNCES TAVERN MUSEUM

Address: 54 Pearl Street

Phone: 212.425.1778

✏️ Directions: R or W to Whitehall Street; 4 or 5 to Bowling
Green; 1 to South Ferry; J, M, or Z to Broad Street

Other details at: www.FrauncesTavernMuseum.org

Anyone with a fetish for the Revolutionary War, early American history, and especially George Washington is in for a very special treat at the Fraunces Tavern Museum, which is not to imply that others will not appreciate it as well. The oldest building in Manhattan, the museum is a historic landmark preserved as it was in its days as a tavern that opened in 1762 by Samuel Fraunces.

First known as The Queen's Head Tavern, the building plays several important roles in New York City's history. Fraunces was known for his cooking, and modern New Yorkers can thank the kitchen at 54 Pearl Street for pioneering take-out service for people who lived in the neighborhood, something we all rely on today. The New York Chamber of Commerce was founded here in 1768. Given its connection to the business community, the tavern served as a hotbed for revolutionary grumbling by merchants angry at the Stamp Act, among other complaints.

However, Fraunces Tavern ultimately captured its special place in history when George Washington stopped by after the British evacuated New York. He hosted a gala at the tavern on November 25, 1783. The tavern was also the site of Washington's famous farewell speech to officers of the Continental Army a few weeks later on December 4.

The museum is two stories tall and is operated by the New York State chapter of the Sons of the Revolution. It contains an entertaining and educational mix of historic re-creations, original and reproduced documents from prominent Revolutionary figures, photographs of historic statues and plaques, and tshatshkes. Visitors can see for themselves what Washington's feast may have been like in the Long Room, recreated in the style of an eighteenth-century public dining room. Across the hall, the Clinton Room, named for the first governor of New York who hosted the infamous Washington party, is decorated with unique "mural" wallpaper.

Upstairs, several glass cases honoring heroes of the Revolution proudly display a range of patriotic paraphernalia. The museum's tribute to Nathan Hale, the patriot Connecticut schoolteacher captured and executed by the British for spying, includes a sliver of wood from a joist of the Nathan Hale School House. A letter from "Brother No. Hale" is also prominently displayed.

The main shrine, though, is dedicated to George Washington. Some artifacts on display include a fragment in a tin case of George Washington's coffin and a chunk of George Washington's pew from St. Paul's Church. If you ever wondered what the man looked like under his powdered wig, here's your answer: A locket of

George Washington's hair encased in a circular glass frame is available for inspection. (Who knew it was reddish brown?) There is also a fragment of one of George's teeth trapped in a locket, under a magnifying glass. The tooth came from George's dentures. (Warning: It is a little on the decayed side.) Since I love relics, this is my favorite part of the museum.

After all the hoopla with the heroes, I was a bit amused to find some less than historical objects on display. In what may be the most pointless museum exhibit ever, there is a shrine to Flag Day amongst all the important ephemera. A glass case is filled with four miniature American flags and two pictures of the Flag Day Parade on June 14, 2001. *Long live Flag Day*, I thought to myself as I surveyed the scene.

Everything else in the museum is a hodgepodge of paintings, portraits, more information on the Sons of the Revolution (it might as well be a museum dedicated to themselves), and other odds and ends. A temporary exhibit, If These Walls Could Talk, covers the history of 54 Pearl Street, from private home to tavern (including the 1762 promissory note Fraunces signed to buy the building) to museum, which the Sons of the Revolution opened in 1907 after a controversial restoration process. Another exhibit, Flash of Color, is an overview of flags in America.

The first floor has been restored as a tavern and restaurant in the spirit of The Queen's Head, if not the menu. (Turtle soup, a display in the museum explains, was huge back then. Today, you'll find hamburgers and arugula salads.) When available, the prix fixe lunch menu is a good deal. T-shirts, mugs, pens shaped like rifles or drum sticks, and cuddly Colonial teddy bears with "Fraunces Tavern Museum" embroidered on their furry tummies are on sale in the restaurant. The merchants who gathered at the site some two hundred years ago would be proud.

On Pearl Street between Wall Street and Broad Street are several **archeological dig sites** exposing seventeenth-century wells and the foundation of a tavern from the late 1600s. Artifacts from Revolutionary times, such as pipes and bowls, were found scattered within the tavern's perimeter. A sign explains the significance of the wells and early New York history. It's an unexpected and cool find in the middle of an otherwise mundane office plaza.

NEW YORK CITY POLICE MUSEUM

Address: 100 Old Slip

Phone: 212.480.3100

Directions: 4 or 5 to Bowling Green; 2 or 3 to Wall Street;
R or W to Whitehall Street; 1 to South Ferry

Other details at: www.NYCPoliceMuseum.org

The New York City Police Museum manages to be historic, ridiculous, and extraordinarily touching at the same time, which is an impressive achievement. The museum is housed in a former police precinct. Standing alone on a little island with a fountain and police cars parked in front, it resembles a fortress. The scene reminds me of those police movies from the 1970s, where the stationhouse is presented as an outpost of the government in hostile territory.

The museum's entryway is restored to the original precinct design. Saunter up to the front desk with your perp in tow . . . and pay your admission. A real, uniformed cop sometimes sits at the desk. If you've ever wanted to reenact an arrest and booking scene from an old movie, here's your chance.

My favorite aspect of the museum is its complete randomness. Everything from old dispatch equipment to police motorcycles to ornamental batons dripping with tassels are on display. Of course, there are tons of guns to admire as well. Signage and explanation of the exhibited items are scattershot at best. You, too, can be a detective as you try to figure out what the hell you are looking at.

Hands down, my favorite display is the second floor case filled with confiscated sinister, but creative, weapons. Baseball bats look much more lethal when a horseshoe is nailed onto the end or when metal spikes are welded all over the bat. An ice pick, nunchucks (or at least I think they were nunchucks), brass knuckles, and other charming instruments of death and destruction are also on display.

A giant camera from 1910 used for mug shots, sometimes done as group photos, is on display close to photos of the accused from the early 1900s. The mug shots are a fascinating revelation about the times. People were allowed to wear their hats in some of the photos, including a woman wearing an enormous black hat and veil that partly obscures her face. The backs of the pictures describe each person's physical characteristics in a matter-of-fact, racist manner.

At the far end of the second floor, a simulated street scene depicts a barbershop pole next to a fortune teller's storefront window. Next door to the fortune teller is a window of a fabric store. Why? I have no idea. A parking meter and lamppost can be found on the periphery of the room, also for no discernable reason.

Interactive elements abound in the museum as well. There's a jail cell in which visitors may pose. (Those unafraid to linger can read about the history of police matrons.) A wall with height markings is available to serve as a background for your own mug shot.

On the top floor of the museum is the Hall of Heroes. I found myself choking up as I read the names of all NYPD officers who died in the line of duty, starting with James Cahill, killed on September 29, 1854. The other major presentation, 9/11 Remembered, keeps the waterworks flowing as an interview with a police dispatcher is shown, along with items recovered from the site. It is extremely well done.

The museum packs a two-story gift shop. Be sure to visit on the way out for all the NYPD paraphernalia you could ever want.

M
A
N
H
A
T
T
A
N

AMERICAN NUMISMATIC SOCIETY/NEW YORK FEDERAL RESERVE BANK

Address: 33 Liberty Street

Phone: 212.571.4470

@→ Directions: 2 or 3 to Wall Street; 4 or 5 to Wall Street; J, M, or Z to Broad Street

Other details at: www.numismatics.org/exhibits/DrachmasDou-bloonsDollars

Anyone who loves money will enjoy the American Numismatic Society's exhibit Drachmas, Dubloons, and Dollars, and the New York Federal Reserve Bank's own interactive museum, Fed Works. Located under arched stone ceilings, leaded glass, and wrought iron in the Fed's stone Renaissance palazzo until the Numismatic Society completes its own building down the street, this exhibit is all about the Benjamins. The objective is to use societies' monetary systems to explain history and culture. As the exhibit's introduction notes, "Money makes the world go round. Money makes the man, and money answers all things."

More than twenty glass cases display coins and paper money, starting in ancient Greece and Egypt, ending in the United States in the twentieth century. Currency from all regions of the world is also displayed. While most coins are round and depict religious or political figures, some of the more interesting items are square (such as a 1600s Swedish copper plate money that was deposited in a bank due to its large size and weight, for which the depositor received a paper note, thus ushering paper money into Europe), shell-shaped (from ancient and medieval Asian countries), or even octagonal (a $50 assayers coin issued during the Gold Rush). It is tempting to smash the glass case and pocket the modern paper bills from around the world.

Many parts of the exhibit are dedicated to the history of minting money in the United States. A wood cabin is plopped between display cases showing ancient and medieval Asian coins. This replica of the 1792 U.S. Mint in Philadelphia contains a mannequin making money by working a 1806 half-and-obverse die. Signs explain the history of minting coins in our fledgling nation. Another display case notes that the new mint had trouble producing enough coins. Short-lived coins from the 1800s (I could only imagine the hassle of carrying around 2¢, 3¢, 20¢, or $3 coins) reminded me that our current denominations came about through trial and error, not unlike throwing spaghetti at the wall and seeing what stuck.

The staid numismatic displays are the perfect lead-in to Fed Works, which is mostly directed at children and features many interactive elements. One machine enables you match wits with none other than Ben Franklin. Another allows you to sit in on a meeting with the Fed's Board of Governors. I learned how multicolored money helps prevent fraud, and then ogled a glass tower with $48 million in shredded hundred dollar bills inside. Tours of the Federal Reserve are available by calling 212.720.6130 or emailing frbnytours@ny.frb.org.

Sadly, this museum has no gift shop or free samples.

All that money leave you hungry, physically and spiritually? **Little Lad's Basket** (120 Broadway, 212.227.5744) is one of my favorite completely unexpected restaurants. Located in the basement of a huge office building just off Wall Street, the vegan eatery is run by Seventh Day Adventists from Maine. Since the place has no meat or dairy, it attracts a people-watching mix of kosher Jews, Muslims, Hindus, hippies, and weirdos like me. The buffet is a mere $3.99 for all the food you can fit into a Styrofoam plate and bowl. Since you can't always bask in the eatery's windowless atmosphere brightened by floor-to-ceiling photographed garden wallpaper, baked goods, granola, and amazing popcorn (made with addictive "herbs") are sold for your home eating pleasure. It is a fun contrast to the homages to capitalism and money at the American Numismatic Society and Museum of American Finance.

MUSEUM OF AMERICAN FINANCE

Address: 48 Wall Street

Phone: 212.908.4110

✏→ Directions: 2 or 3 to Wall Street; 4 or 5 to Wall Street;
J or M to Broad Street; 1 to Rector Street; R or W to
Rector Street

Other details at: www.FinancialHistory.org

I love one-room museums, especially ones with attendant gift shops that are approximately the same size as the museum's exhibits, so I was disappointed that the former Museum of American Financial History moved from a two-room hole in the wall to a 30,000-square-foot historic former bank. However, the new space certainly is a more fitting place in which to celebrate the glorious excess of American financial markets.

Housed in the former Bank of New York building (a structure dissected at the Skyscraper Museum), the permanent exhibits are dedicated to financial markets, money, banking, and entrepreneurship. Objects of note from the museum's former home include a plate for printing bank notes and securities, a ticker tape machine that prints personal messages for visitors, and "seats" from the trading floor of the Stock Exchange. Other interesting items: an original ticker tape from October 29, 1929, saved by a broker in Boston, and the last "emergency cash" check signed by a president. (In the days before ATMs, presidents would bring these along on their travels.) The fifth and coolest exhibit is the Alexander Hamilton room, which is decorated in the style of his period and features artifacts from the first Secretary of the United States Treasury.

The building itself is a museum-quality restoration of a 1927 bank. Murals depicting industry, trade, and banking flank the side walls, and the three murals on the front wall framing the exhibit on financial markets tell the story of the founding of the Bank of New York. The best part? Telescopes are strategically placed around the floor so that you can get a close look at the wonderful details in the murals. A section of the old teller booths remain, and the gift shop is off to the side behind gorgeous wrought iron bars.

The gift shop sells various knickknacks, antiques, books about finance, jewelry, ties, statues and sculptures, New York paraphernalia, and exorbitantly priced posters.

It's never too early for some brew at **Jeremy's Ale House** (228 Front Street, 212.964.3537), known for its 8 a.m. happy hour. Join cops as they leave the third watch and guzzle their cares away. Wash down an egg and cheese on a roll with "The Eye Opener" (cheap buckets of original Coors). Jeremy's believes that "beer isn't just for breakfast anymore." If you do go later in the day, expect to revel with stockbrokers celebrating their latest robbery of Joe citizen. Jeremy's original location was known for its "décor" of ties chopped off lucky brokers' necks and abandoned bras tacked onto the wall and ceiling fixtures. They've moved a few times within a few blocks on Front Street, and the most recent location seems to be trying a bit too hard to reach the same heights of taste, but if you're drunk enough, you may not even notice.

THE LOWER EAST SIDE TROLL MUSEUM

Address: 122 Orchard Street
E-mail: revjen@revjen.com
Directions: F to Delancy Street; M to Essex Street
Other Details at: www.revjen.com
Appointments are required.

Located in the 6th floor walk-up apartment of its founder
and curator, a petite brunette performance artist and
Lower East Side enthusiast by the *nom de guerre* Reverend Jen Miller, a trip to the Lower East Side Troll
Museum is a visit to an alternative universe. Given its
function as both home and museum, all visits to the Troll
Museum must be scheduled in advance; otherwise, the
curator warns potential visitors that she "might be busy
having sex." A Sunday afternoon phone call was all it took
to secure an appointment for the following day. According
to Reverend Jen, there is a suggested donation of "$3,000,
but only for Japanese tourists who don't know better." The
museum is free to all others.

Eagerly anticipating my visit, I arrived with three
friends a few minutes before our 7:00 p.m. booking. As we
killed time observing the vibrant street life, Reverend Jen
and her chihuahua, the Reverend Jen Jr. (a.k.a. JJ, "a living
troll"), approached. Quickly deducing that we were waiting patrons of the museum, Reverend Jen requested that

we kindly remain downstairs until she put on her elf ears, a crucial element for our "proper Troll Museum education." We obliged, and thus received the "Secret Passcode" to buzz for entry.

The Troll Museum occupies the first one hundred square feet or so of Rev. Jen's approximately 300-square-foot apartment. Psychedelic reds, blues, and greens adorn the walls, forming a perfect backdrop for displaying multitudes of big-haired trolls and troll memorabilia dating from the 1960s to 1990s.

Our tour began with Reverend Jen's very first troll, Adrianna (a medium-sized troll whose head, unfortunately, became removable). Reverend Jen then covered everything from the rare and one-of-a-kind double-headed troll to a small sample of the 750 varieties of trolls mass produced by Russ toy company in the 1990s. The museum also offers special exhibits following more mainstream museum trends. When the Guggenheim offered Armani at the Guggenheim in 2000, the Troll Museum staged Armani at the Troll Museum, displaying a collection of troll couture exclusively designed by Reverend Jen and friends.

The Troll Museum welcomes donations for the permanent collection. Admirers of Reverend Jen contribute trolls of all kinds. One donation displayed is a mini troll crucified on a piece of wood. When I asked about it, Reverend Jen noted, "People send me a lot of disturbing objects."

Videos, coloring books, and portraits painted by Reverend Jen complete this original museum. On one panel of her diptych self-portrait, a young Reverend Jen dreams of being an artist, and a magical troll grants her wish. In the other panel, the troll reveals that such fame will only come after she is no longer living, and that she will die alone and miserable. The portrait illustrates that while trolls are generally thought to bring good luck, they can sometimes be vindictive, Reverend Jen explained. (Also, it is a great example of her sense of humor.)

Photos courtesy of Troll Museum

Although museum aficionados must order any souvenirs online, onsite display items include Troll Museum beer cozies, T-shirts, and trolls with little ribbons that read "Reverend Jen Loves Me."

What is the Lower East Side if not pickled? Find out for yourself at the **Pickle Guys** (49 Essex Street, 212-656-9739). The Pickle Guys are one of two LES pickle makers producing pickles in the traditional way. According to staff, horseradish is grated daily, and employees wear gas masks to complete the task. Pickles come in many varieties; grab a sour one and munch away. Pickle alternative: **Guss' Pickles** (85-87 Orchard Street, 212-334-3616) operating (with a slight interruption to move from Essex to Orchard) since 1910, is preferred by many pickle aficionados. Taste test at both and decide for yourself.

• • • • • • • • • • •

Every day is Halloween at **Economy Candy** (108 Rivington Street, 800.352.4544). This store of wonders bills itself as the "Nosher's Paradise of the Lower East Side" and definitely lives up to its name. All kinds of candy, nuts, and dried fruit are sold by the pound. In addition, there is a random selection of teas, packaged treats, and other small grocery items that are hard to find elsewhere. If I want a kind of candy that I haven't seen in the last decade in any normal store, I know I can buy it here. (And it somehow won't be stale, either.) Candy cigarettes or cigars? No problem! Economy Candy has been infuriating dentists and the politically correct since 1937. You can also buy vintage gumball machines and other cool tshatshkes.

• • • • • • • • • • •

If you are caught up in the Jewish history of the neighborhood (or just want to flee the yuppie influx), try an old favorite and head over to **Yonah Schimmel's Knishery** (137 E. Houston, 212.477.2858). Yonah Schimmel himself, who glares at you from a black-and- white photo by the register, did not offer as many varieties of knish when the shop first opened in 1910 as they do today, but all are damn tasty. I swear that the tables are serviced by people who were at the grand opening of the store, but this just adds to the experience in my humble opinion. Excuse my sweet potato fetish, but I do believe that they make some fine knish filling. Try a traditional potato knish if you are a purist. Desserts are also available.

NEW YORK CITY FIRE MUSEUM

Address: 278 Spring Street
Phone: 212.691.1303
→ Directions: C or E to Spring Street; 1 to Houston Street
Other details at: www.NYCFireMuseum.org

If you like your museums in authentic settings, then the New York City Fire Museum is right up your fire pole. The building served as a New York City firehouse from 1905–1950. Since 1987, it has been a museum chock-full of volunteer former and current firefighters.

I recommend resisting the urge to start in the room with all the fire engines. First, head over to the small display on the history of firefighting, which is more or less behind the large gift shop. For the most part, none of the objects have dates, but the antique equipment (fire syringe, anyone?) reminded me why small fires used to burn down entire cities hundreds of years ago. Interesting items include decorated personal buckets used to throw water on fires from the 1800s and a linen "salvage bag" that was used by firemen to carry out items from a burning building (often prioritized over putting out the fire).

Next, head over to the main exhibit. The room is full of equipment and trucks. An array of sharp and blunt tools from the 1900s amply displays how firemen scrambled up walls, including a life gun that shot a line of rope up to a roof. Firefighting gear (coats, boots, and helmets) in both adult and child sizes are available to try on.

Did I mention that there are also horse-drawn and automated fire trucks to check out? The museum is the proud home to one of the oldest fire engines on the continent, the Farnam-style engine. The Farnam was built in New York around 1790 and constituted a vast improvement over buckets, with two arms that were pumped up and down to draw out water. While the majority of steam fire engines that once existed in the U.S. were destroyed in the scrap drives of World War II, you can not only see a 1901 LaFrance steam engine from Brooklyn, but also a 1912 steamer with a gas-powered Van Blerck tractor, which marked the transition from horse-drawn to gas-powered fire engines.

The museum also honors non-human firefighters. The role and history of horses in New York's firehouses are illustrated with photos. (I learned that the first FDNY ambulance was for injured horses, not people.) Firehouse dogs are also given their due, with photos of companies with their dogs on display. Chief, the actual stuffed and mounted hero dog of Brooklyn's Engine Company 203, bravely stands alert under the portraits. After wondering into the firehouse in 1929, Chief rescued hundreds of people alongside the firefighters. He was hit by a car and killed in 1939.

Upstairs are more fire trucks, but mostly information and paraphernalia related to parades. It seems that parades were a huge deal back in the early days of firefighting in New York, giving volunteer brigades a chance to show off their equipment and fancy costumes. Badges, posters, medallions, hats, and special wagon decorations from the parades are all presented. In addition to the engines, the museum has four-wheeled hose reels. The competitive Steinway Hose No. 7 and Astoria Hose No. 8 from Queens are especially splendidly decked out.

The stairwell to the third floor is decorated with 433 patches left behind from visiting firefighters after 9/11. Back on the first floor, Kleenex is supplied throughout a gut-wrenching 9/11 memorial. I knew that if I saw this exhibit first, it would make it hard to enjoy the rest of the museum, and I was right. Save it for last.

Don't let your emotions dictate your spending in the gift shop on your way out, although it is chock-full of fun items. Anything you could possibly want relating to firefighting or the FDNY specifically—toys, patches, clothes, bags, stuffed animals, hats, key chains, and so forth—are sold by friendly firefighters.

Indulge your sweet tooth at the futuristic **Rice to Riches** *(37 Spring Street, 212.274.0008). Offering dozens of flavors of rice pudding (such as chocolate, mascarpone, banana, and cinnamon) with a toppings bar, the shop has something for everyone. Bowls are specially designed plastic pods and the spoons are funky long sticks, both perfect to take home and use again. The setting is surreal, with techno music and video screens displaying flashing images while people stand at curvy counters or sit in podlike booths.*

DIA CENTER FOR THE ARTS: THE NEW YORK EARTH ROOM AND THE BROKEN KILOMETER

Address: 141 Wooster Street (The New York Earth Room) and 393 West Broadway (The Broken Kilometer)

Phone: 212.989.5566 (Dia main number)

⟶ Directions: R or W to Prince Street; B, D, V, or F to Broadway - Lafayette; C or E to Spring Street; 6 to Spring Street

Other details at: www.EarthRoom.org and www.BrokenKilometer.org

Real estate in New York City is almost always at a premium. The prime locations of the Dia's two SoHo art installations by Walter De Maria made me feel that the works were extra avant-garde because of where they are. They are sticks in the eyes of the real estate market.

Described by the Dia as "an interior earth sculpture," The New York Earth Room was created in 1977. The work is housed in a nondescript building (I'm guessing a former factory or warehouse) with an extremely unwelcoming metal door, reminiscent of where Patrick Swayze and Demi Moore lived in the movie *Ghost*. It is essentially a very large white-walled room with naked light bulbs, full of dirt. In fact, there are 250 cubic yards of earth, 22 inches deep, covering 3,600 square feet of floor space. As I stood in the doorway and looked at what could easily be a $1.5 million loft, the dirt pile reached up to my knees. The

280,000 pounds of dirt are raked and watered once a week, according to the guy behind the desk.

The Broken Kilometer, installed by De Maria in 1979, is only slightly less ridiculous. Taking up valuable store-front space on trendy West Broadway are 500 "highly polished, round, solid brass rods, each measuring two meters in length and five centimeters in diameter." The whole work is 125 feet long (it definitely gets less light in the back) by 45 feet wide, interrupted by white structural columns. You can contemplate all five rows of 100 rods from a bench at the front of the room. Like The New York Earth Room, the white-walled room with light wood floors is a quiet and bizarre setting in the midst of trendy, bustling Soho.

MUSEUM OF COMIC AND CARTOON ART (MOCCA)

Address: 594 Broadway, #401

Phone: 212.254.3511

Directions: B, D, F, or V to Broadway - Lafayette; 6 to Bleeker
    Street; R or W to Prince Street

Other details at: www.MoccaNY.org

The Museum of Comic and Cartoon Art (MoCCA) is a one-room museum with a can-do spirit. The permanent collection's pieces range from political cartoons (including a WWII anti-Japanese illustration depicting a soldier venerating his Hitler-mustached ancestor by Crockett Johnson, who wrote one of my favorite childhood books, *Harold and the Purple Crayon*) to pages from graphic novels to Sunday comic strips. Noteworthy items include a drawing of a Nazi boy soldier by Mary Stewart, the only woman artist (and the sister of actor Jimmy Stewart) included in a 1942 show about the Axis powers; a strip from Alison Bechdel's awesome "Dykes to Watch Out For;" and work from a Baby Sitters Club graphic novel by Queens artist Regina Telgemeier.

Animation also abounds. The museum has a small Warner Bros. collection. There's a 1982 cel of Daffy Duck, drawings of Bugs Bunny in a blonde wig wearing a very pointy carrot bra (perhaps Madonna's "Blonde Ambition" inspiration?), and a drawing and watercolor of the infamous Warner Bros.' episode "Tortoise Wins by a Hare."

However, my personal favorites are the pencil sketch and cel from the Powerpuff Girls "Abrac-Cadaver" episode.

Two flat-panel TVs play animation continuously. The TV near the entrance silently shows cartoons and pictures of political commentary and propaganda from World War II. The other TV plays silent cartoons from the early 1900s. Be sure to catch the sly 'toon from 1912 about a mosquito harassing a guy.

MoCCA is rounded out with small changing exhibits that are not physically separate from the permanent collection and a long reading table in the center of the room. People are welcome to stay to read the materials about the exhibits and other books about cartooning.

The gift shop could be better, but it offers some obscure comic books (natch), videos, and postcards.

UKRAINIAN MUSEUM

Address: 222 E. 6th Street

Phone: 212.228.0110

@, Directions: 6 to Astor Place; R or W to 8th Street - NYU;
       F or V to 2nd Avenue

Other details at: www.UkrainianMuseum.org

There is one reason to go to the Ukrainian Museum, and you can see half of it in the window facing the street: *pysanka* (a.k.a. Easter eggs). My friend Des and I dealt with the surly Eastern European staff member collecting admission at the front desk just so we could get a closer look at these jewels. The hollowed-out egg shells are painted with elaborate geometric patterns, animals like deer and chickens, and flowers and trees. Hanging from strings, the oval objects shine as light hits the glossy brown, red, ochre, and forest green paints primarily used. Different regions have slightly different pysanka motifs, but the decorated egg tradition stems from pre-Christian times as a spring ritual celebrating the rebirth of nature. The oldest egg on display is from 1868.

Just because the pysanka are the best thing about the museum doesn't mean that there is nothing else to see, though. A permanent collection of Ukrainian art focuses on twentieth-century sculpting and painting. Not that I am a modern art expert, but the works seem much more centered around Christian themes than other art that I am familiar with from that period.

The lower level has an exhibit comparing the patterns and designs in pysanka to those found in Ukrainian embroidery. Richly decorated shirts from as early as 1900 are placed side-by-side with eggs. The eggs tend to have only one repeating motif, whereas the clothing has more than one. Some of the shirts had such huge collars they seemed to be the progenitors to today's ubiquitous hoodie.

You can bring home a pysanka for as little as $20 from the gift shop. The store also sells cards, embroidered linens and pillows, traditional clothes, teddy bears in traditional clothes, dolls, books, and jewelry.

Street artist James De La Vega holds court at his art store, **Galeria De La Vega** (102 St. Marks Place, 212.876.8649). Chairs with thought-provoking phrases painted on them (such as "Blacks Only") invite conversation with the sunglass-wearing artist. De La Vega is known for his pithy slogans in English and Spanish (e.g., "Become your dream," "Don't let idiots ruin your day," "Sometimes the king is a woman"), which you can buy printed on everything from stickers to mugs to T-shirts. Browse his infamous sketch series, "My Mother as . . ." which depicts his mother as famous people such as Elvis, Frida Kahlo, Castro, Madonna, Marilyn Manson, and not famous people like the hilarious "My Mother Refusing to Help Children" or "My Mother as Dog Balls."

Speaking of dog balls, if you are in the market for odd objects like teeth, a stuffed armadillo, or Victorian hats, head over to **Obscura Antiques** (280 E. 10th Street, 212.505.9251) pronto. Glass cases are filled with antique enema syringes, anatomical models, and outdated books on sexuality. Mounted preserved fish and birds grace the walls next to a poster-size framed photo of an old woman in a coffin. Porcelain dolls (some headless and stuffed in jars) share shelf space with what looks like Aunt Erma's beloved dead cat. Yes, Victorian clothing and Mason and Shriner hats are the most normal items in the shop. "It's a mix between a medical history museum, a taxidermist, and a Victorian haberdashery," my friend Des noted.

FORBES GALLERIES

Address: 62 Fifth Avenue

Phone: 212.206.5548

Directions: 4, 5, 6, L, N, Q, R, or W to 14th Street - Union Square; F or V to 14th Street; 1, 2, or 3 to 14th Street

Other details at: www.ForbesGalleries.com

Malcolm Forbes Jr. was a wealthy man. As we all know, the rich very much love their toys. Forbes's fondness for playthings—miniature boats, games, soldiers—continued throughout his life. Fortunately for us little people, he decided to share his goodies and thoughts via the Forbes Galleries. Signage throughout the museum is full of witty and warm reflections on toys from Forbes that are a pleasure to read. As a result, the Forbes Galleries is one of the most fun museums in the City.

After passing a small lobby showcasing the eight versions of the Forbes's family yacht, *The Highlander* (including their indignant response to the closing of a tax loop that forced them to actually pay for something they personally owned and used for pleasure—the nerve!); an oil painting of the Forbes family lounging at poolside (the boys playing with boats), and several art deco panels taken from *The Normandie*, a 1935 French oceanliner billed as "a floating museum of decorative arts" before it was seized by the US to be used as a troop carrier, I entered Ships Ahoy, an exhibit of toy boats that makes me want a chocolate chip cookie every time I think about it. Forbes's notes in the gallery remind us that his collection of World War I–era toy boats is especially rare because not only did the metal boats rust, but it was not so easy to recover a sunken boat from oceans and lakes during seaside play as it was from a bathtub. Many good toy ships wound up "lost at sea."

Forbes also cheerfully and patiently explains the difference between a toy boat and a model boat, something visitors should keep in mind as they eyeball dozens of warships, ocean liners, sailboats, and my favorite, submarines. The menacing submarines patrol a narrow, dark case, suspended at various depths in the murky waters surrounded by deep-sea divers in heavy helmets, sunken ships, and metal sharks. The mysteriously threatening display captured my imagination.

Another fantastic exhibit contains an old copper and wooden bathtub filled with "bubbles" and toy boats. A box of Titanic Soap ("Guaranteed to sink!" the box boasts) is in the metal soap dish attached to the tub. Surrounding the tub are Victorian-era wooden Noah's arks with herds of animals ready to board each ship. Some of the arks more resemble large barns than something that might take to water successfully. (I suspect the unicorns boarded those vessels.) Magnetic floating toys sit in a fancy box at the foot of the tub.

Back on dry land, the On Parade exhibit contains thousands of toy soldiers. Forbes explains the history of toy soldiers, which began as flat, tin cutouts, and the different companies that manufactured them. The soldiers are arranged in a series of tableaus in their display cases, generally representing an important moment in history. Julius Caesar and Cleopatra lead a progression as Kaiser Wilhelm and his wife review Prussian troops on horseback. Toy soldiers recreate the 1935 Italian invasion of Ethiopia. King George and Queen Mary permanently endure their coronation. Flat Aztec warriors do battle with the forces of Cortés on a pyramid in 1521 in a central display case. An English fox hunt silently proceeds as William Tell stands frozen with an apple on his head. Finally, 1,400 pieces that are twenty millimeters tall continue to fight the 1870 Franco-Prussian War.

In the next part of the exhibit, civilian dolls are set on moving ramps. Music accompanies the figures as they are perpetually whisked around in circles. One display has marchers from different eras set against pictures of cities and villages around the world. Suffragettes demand the right to vote. A guy with a sandwich board reading, "Buy Forbes," cruised by me as I pressed my face to the glass for a closer look at the samples of humanity on parade. Across the aisle, pioneers in the Wild West fight Native Americans encircling them on horseback.

The only interactive part of the museum is intriguingly bizarre. Snippets of Robert Louis Stevenson's poem "Land of Counterpane" are displayed. The poem is about a sick kid playing in bed with his toys, and Forbes set up a life-size diorama in the museum. Visitors can stick their heads into the scene and imagine themselves as the sick child. I followed in the footsteps of Lech Walesa and Ronald Reagan, individually pictured laughing with their heads in the box, when I stuck mine in there, too.

A capitalist like Forbes can't resist the game of Monopoly. The Monopoly exhibit traces the folk origins of the game from an early 1920s version called The Landlord's Game. The Landlord's Game is carved into a thick wooden plank, hand painted, and laid out similarly to what we recognize as a modern Monopoly board with spaces admonishing players to "Go to Jail" or pay taxes. The longer I looked at it, the more I thought this was a very hardscrabble and punitive view of the world—it's almost impossible to overcome the system. I wondered if it was a socialist game in this incarnation. The first "modern" Monopoly sets were hand painted onto oil cloth, with the deeds and cards all individually typed. A 1932 version first sets the game in Atlantic City, and two 1933 versions are also on display. One is recognizable as the game we have in our living rooms, albeit more crudely made, and the other is on a round "board." The Monopoly collection is rounded out with a 1972 hand-drawn cardboard game of "Oligopoly," consisting of Forbes's properties and magazine titles, and modern Monopoly sets from Russia, Italy, France, and Germany.

Wind your way through the last exhibit, The Mortality of Immortality, the most randomly stocked gallery. Forbes illustrates how we commemorate our deeds with displays of plaques, trophies, photos, posters, and medals. More unusual *objects d'memory* include deer feet made into a fork and knife, other stuffed animals, and random sports equipment. The glass on part of this display is designed to emulate a pawn shop façade. I guess the implication is that even great people may face hard times and need to pawn their treasures and monuments to themselves.

The museum actually also has odds and ends sprinkled throughout, such as a crayon drawing of a boat done by Forbes at age eight; paintings of fisherman, sailors, and boys; and paraphernalia from toy boat companies. There's no gift shop, which is most unfortunate. I bet they would have had some great souvenir toys.

The most whimsical, witty subway station is doubtless found at the **14th Street A,C,E platform**. Graced by the 2000 Tom Otterness installation, Life Underground, the station's riders share space with little bronze sculptures centered around—what else?—money. Reminiscent of the round-headed guy from Monopoly games, the figures poke fun at life in New York. Check under a stairway, and there's an alligator emerging from the sewer, grabbing a guy with a money bag for a head. Under another stairway, a lobster with a money bag head clutches a man and woman in each claw. A mouse nibbles on a coin from a broken change bag while other critters hang from the rafters. Take a seat on the bench in the middle of the platform facing the local track, and you'll find yourself next to a roly-poly man holding a money bag, looking anxiously uptown.

Courtesy of Stef Weiss

MIDDLE

·

MANHATTAN

THEODORE ROOSEVELT'S BIRTHPLACE

Address: 28 E. 20th Street
Phone: 212.260.1616
Directions: 6 to 23rd Street; R or W to 23rd Street
Other details at: www.nps.gov/thrb/

In general, I don't like recreated historic places nearly as much as I like the originals. I tend to feel slightly cheated that I'm not standing at the *actual* place that so-and-so famous person also stood at. The Theodore Roosevelt Birthplace is a delightful exception to my rule.

The original home of the Roosevelt family was demolished in the early 1900s. After TR died, his family hired a female (!) architect to rebuild the structure as it was in 1865. Sixty-five percent of the furniture that was used to refurnish the replica house is what was originally in there, including Teddy's special, little red velvet chair (built for him because the horsehair covering on the other parlor room furniture irritated him), his parents' hand-carved bedroom set (including the bed he was born in), and the enormous polished dining room table. Guided tours of the house are given by United States Park Rangers and volunteers every hour. The tour is the only way to see the entire property, so plan your visit accordingly.

While Roosevelt is known for implementing progressive policies in the United States, he is also famous for his avid love of hunting, and this site does not shy away from his hobby. In a second-floor gallery only accessible through the tour, numerous trophies are on display, including two birds stuffed by TR when he was only ten years old. Larger prizes include an elephant foot, a lion, and a mounted bear head.

The site also contains a trove of objects from Teddy's life that can be viewed on your own. Among the items on display in what I classify as the "papers category" are letters to a sickly young TR from his dad, TR's diary from his childhood trip to Europe written in his handwriting, a miniscule diary in which a young TR recorded his daily exercises, and a legislative diary lamenting corruption from his days in Albany. Items falling into the "fiber category" include TR's christening gown, his parents' wedding clothes (the corset his mother wore indicates that she must have been something like a size 0), and, most fascinating, the shirt that Teddy was wearing when he was the victim of an assassination attempt. The white shirt is marred by a tiny bullet hole and is displayed with the shot-through text of a speech that he was preparing to deliver, as well as the glasses case that probably saved his life by deflecting the bullet. (He refused immediate medical treatment and went on to deliver the speech in full before going to the hospital.)

A gift corner in the lobby consists of a small table with tshatshkes such as TR bendy dolls (think Gumby), postcards, pocket books on teddy bears, and books and videos about Roosevelt.

Since 1929, **Eisenberg's Sandwich Shop** (174 Fifth Avenue, 212.675.5096) has been serving tasty deli sandwiches and comfort food like meat loaf. Although the lunch counter has a new owner, not much else has changed since then, including the staff. A room was recently added to the back of the restaurant so more than two people can dine together, but the charm lies at the counter. Grab a stool and hang out while the short-order cooks assemble the creamiest egg, tuna, and chicken salad sandwiches known to man. For a meatier fix, get the pastrami on rye and wash it down with an egg cream. Yum.

MASONIC HALL AND THE CHANCELLOR ROBERT R. LIVINGSTON LIBRARY AND MUSEUM OF GRAND LODGE

Address: 71 W. 23rd Street

Phone: 212.337.6620

Directions: F to 23rd Street; 1, 2, or 3 to 23rd Street;
     R or W to 23rd Street

Other details at: www.NYMasonicLibrary.org

I always wanted to learn the ancient secrets of the Masons. Might my mission be accomplished with a visit to the Masonic Hall and the Chancellor Robert R. Livingston Masonic Library and Museum of Grand Lodge?

As I trudged through the slushy streets of Manhattan on a gray day in March, I worried a bit that my outing could not possibly live up to my expectations. However, as soon as I was in the Masonic Hall with its elaborately decorated lobby, I knew I would not be disappointed. Even better, as I stepped on the elevator to the library, I noticed that there are *free tours* of the building daily. Oh, yes! This trip was shaping up quite nicely.

The library and museum have a delightful collection of weird artifacts, beginning in the hallway. I immediately gravitated to the display case with ginormous scary swords. I learned that in Freemasonry, swords are symbols of intellect, "cutting through veils of superstition and rumor with the fine edge of reason." Well, the Masons certainly know a lot about rumor and superstition, I smugly thought. I was sad to note, though, that swords are generally not used in the "Standard Work" of the Grand Lodge of New York State, although a Mason known as the Tiler (who guards the Lodge door) does carry one as a symbol of his title. (Perhaps to scare the living daylights out of anyone who tries to sneak in to steal their ritual secrets?)

The hallway also displays other random items, such as pitchers, carved walking sticks, pipes, and a mirror, all from the 1800s–1900s and decorated with Masonic symbols. Most notable are two wooden cases, one containing a gavel with a handwritten note explaining that the gavel stone was made from Solomon's quarry in Jerusalem and that the handle is "shithin wood from the wilderness of Judea." Cool. The other box holds a pouch and two bottles, as well as a handwritten note from the U.S. Consul in Jerusalem, Palestine, dated January 19, 1887. The note certifies that "the wine and oil . . . were made in Jerusalem, that the wheat was raised here, and that the leather bottles as are such [illegible] here, and were made in this country. The wine is known as Jerusalem wine, and is seven years old."

I went inside the library, and was cheerfully greeted by the library director. He showed me around and explained some of the other objects to me. Repeatedly, the director stated that the Masons have no secrets, except, of course, the process of making a man a Mason through the conferral of degrees. Unprompted, he assured me that they were not a cult or Satanic. In fact, Masons organize themselves around principles of character and morality using the framework of the legend of the construction of Solomon's Temple.

The little museum and library is chock-to-the-brim full of everything from "bric-a-brac" (the library director's words) such as ashtrays and figurines to surreal paintings with floating eyes and primitive construction tools called "tracing boards" that are used to teach conferees about the Masonic symbols. It holds "jewels" (badges worn by Masons to signify their titles), displays stained glass windows from a former Lodge that closed, and presents autographed pictures of famous Masons, such as astronaut Buzz Aldrin. ("He's the first Mason to walk on the moon," the director enthusiastically noted.) Taking a close look at everything took the better part of two hours, and while I was highly entertained and thoroughly educated, I did not learn the secret rites of the Masons at the library and museum.

Still, I had some hope. A quick trip up to the executive offices of the Grand Lodge revealed two sphinx statues guarding the entryway. Several display cases indicate which leaders throughout American history have been Masons (George Washington and Ben Franklin were Masons) and who were not (Ulysses S. Grant and Robert E. Lee, although their fathers were). In addition, there is a photo gallery of recipients of the Grand Lodge Award of Distinction. I was fascinated to see that Michael A. Richards (a.k.a. Kramer on *Seinfeld*), the creator of the cartoon dog Marmaduke, Red Skelton, John Glenn, Gen.

William Bratton, and Gen. Douglas MacArthur shared the award over the years.

Finally, it was time for the tour of the lodges. A gentleman approximately 150 years of age inserted his hearing aid and took me through several of the Lodge rooms at Masonic Hall. As we visited the elaborately decorated and mysterious rooms, he explained to me multiple times that it was okay to touch things and I should ask him any questions, as they had no secrets and were not a cult. Contrary to what I learned in the library, my friendly tour guide also insisted in his thick Eastern European accent that he was lucky to be in the United States because, unlike those in Europe, the Masons here believe in equality. "That's why we are lucky that Masons wrote the Constitution," he concluded.

Each Lodge has a platform at one end with a niche displaying the Masonic "G" behind a giant chair, an altar of some sort in the middle of the room, benches on each side, an organ at the other end, and to the right of the organ, framing the door, stand two tall columns with

Courtesy of the Livingston Masonic Library

globes on top. Lodges are independently run and each one has its own theme. I visited the Colonial Room (notable for having chairs instead of benches and silver chandeliers); the French Ionic Room (known for its portraits of George Washington and the Marquis de Lafayette, as well as French coats of arms painted on the walls); the Empire Room (with gold-leaf walls); the Gothic Room (modeled after the Saint-Chapelle in Paris with stained glass windows); and the Chapter Room (done in an ancient Egyptian motif and the only room with curtains that divide the room into sections for the "Royal Arch Degrees"). The best room I saw, hands down, is the Grand Lodge Meeting Room, which my guide told me is an exact replica of the ballroom on the *Titanic*, and was built to memorialize "all the victims who drowned." I don't fully understand the connection, but the sentiments are nice and the room is pretty damn cool.

I had to leave before I could enter every Lodge, but it is definitely worth a trip back, even if there is no Masons gift shop selling jewels, swords, or tasseled hats.

CHAPEL OF SACRED MIRRORS (COSM)

Address: 542 W. 27th Street, 4th Floor

Phone: 212.564.4253

Directions: C or E to 23rd Street

Other details at: www.cosm.org

The first thing I discovered at the Chapel of Sacred Mirrors (COSM) is that there are no physical mirrors, which
was initially disappointing. Instead, there are nineteen
framed paintings of full-sized human figures by artist
Alex Grey. Each portrait is interesting in its own way. Some
are famous religious figures, such as Jesus or a Hindu god;
a few are regular naked folks; others are fleshless bundles
of bones, nerves, and muscles; and the remaining ones are
surrounded by energy fields of various sorts. By "mirror-
ing" the paintings' anatomical and religious themes, I was
supposed to see a reflection of myself.

This is a fine metaphysical concept, except that I am
clearly not mature enough to connect to the cosmos
through these mirrors. Instead, I spent the majority of my
time in the chapel comparing the penis sizes of the
African man, the Caucasian man, and the Asian man. All
three appeared to be approximately the same, slightly
unrealistic size. (Not that I am an expert on penis size, but
I am pretty sure that I learned in a college human sexuality course that the average flaccid penis is about three

inches long. These puppies were probably a good five to six inches, extending halfway down each figure's hairy thigh.) I also noted with approval that all three human women had bushy tufts of pubic hair.

A second gallery exhibits Grey's nonmirror works. Like the portraits in the Chapel, these paintings emphasize spirituality and anatomy. Many of the works are sexual in nature, such as the painting of a fleshless man and woman copulating. Another semi-creepy one has a fleshless woman and man French kissing. (Really, I never wondered what someone's tongue would look like in another person's mouth if I could see through their cheeks.) My favorite work in this gallery is a psychedelic altarpiece about Jesus that incorporates themes of science (little portraits of Freud, Curie, Crick & Watson, and Copernicus surround Jesus) and religion (the heads of St. Teresa and St. Augustine mirror the science guys), as well as political leaders (Martin Luther King, Jr. and Gandhi pop up). Swirling around in the background are scenes of human catastrophe and people hanging out with aliens. Very interesting, indeed.

The gift shop sells a video about the sacred mirrors, postcards, incense, rocks, candles, and clothing from Tibet and India. Books about Alex Grey and other topics, such as LSD and East Asian religions, are also available. The Microcosm Gallery sells small original art works by other artists at very reasonable prices. If you want more, anyone can come celebrate the Full Moon and/or New Moon in monthly ceremonies.

HORTICULTURAL SOCIETY OF NEW YORK

Address: 148 W. 37th Street, 13th Floor

Phone: 212.757.0915

Directions: B, D, F, N, Q, R, V, or W to 34th Street - Herald Square; 1, 2, or 3 to 34th Street - Penn Station

Other details at: www.hsny.org

Flora lovers rejoice! Founded in 1900, the Horticultural Society seeks "to improve the quality of life in New York through horticulture." In 1924, the Society added a library, alive and growing today with books. Anyone who thinks of libraries as stuffy will be pleased to find over-sized windows with rows of plants filling the entire floor with light and air.

The public can peruse everything from oversized tomes in Latin (six volumes of *Genera Et Species Plantarium Argentinarum* were on a U-shaped conference table with a sign saying DO NOT TOUCH during my visit) to picture books for kids to gardening journals. All in all, the library houses nearly 12,000 books and bound periodicals. While anyone is welcome to browse, borrowing privileges accrue only to members. Author talks are offered throughout the year.

The Horticultural Society also hosts changing art exhibits in its eco-friendly space. It's a quiet and relaxing retreat from the din of the city.

M
A
N
H
A
T
T
A
N

UNITED NATIONS SCULPTURE GARDEN

Address: United Nations Plaza, First Avenue and 46th Street
Phone: none

Directions: 4, 5, 6, 7, or Shuttle from 42nd Street - Times Square to Grand Central - 42nd Street; 6 to 51st Street

While the garden never seems to be open and it is impossible to get information about when and whether it will ever be, there are many fascinating sculptures that can be observed from the street. My personal favorite is the life-size bronze bull elephant. He resides in the northwest corner of the garden, his ass facing 48th Street. When the bush surrounding the elephant is trimmed, his two-foot-long penis is clearly visible. Other notable sculptures include a large gun tied into a knot and something that seems to be a life-size shipwreck.

Someday, I assume that the garden will be open again and numerous other sculptural treasures will be available to enjoy up close. Until then, walking the gated perimeter for entertainment will have to suffice.

A **waterfall walkway** seems like an unlikely attraction in the middle of Manhattan's business district, and yet it exists. Walk down 48th or 49th Street between Broadway and 6th Avenue, and you'll come to a plaza with a waterfall cascading down a wall. A tunnel with a glass ceiling lets people cut through the wall while water pours overhead. The plaza also has a nifty plaque that thanks the laborers whose toil is responsible for the plaza's construction.

The **Berlin Wall** lives—or at least a section of it, anyway—at a plaza on 53rd Street between 5th and Madison Avenues. Office workers on a cigarette break stand nonchalantly in front of five panels covered with graffiti. There's no explanation why the wall is in this plaza in Manhattan, which makes it all the stranger.

Suzanne Reisman

M
A
N
H
A
T
T
A
N

TOURNEAU GALLERY OF TIME AND ORIS EXHIBIT HALL

Address: 12 E. 57th Street

Phone: 212.758.7300

Directions: F to 57th Street; N, R, W, 4, 5,
or 6 to Lexington Avenue - 59th Street

Tucked away in the basement of the mammoth Tourneau flagship watch store is a mini museum dedicated to Tourneau timepieces. Mostly displaying old ads and men's and women's watches over the past one hundred years, the museum pays homage to luxury watches. I thought the best items are the "disguised" clocks—time pieces inserted, for example, on the tops of lipstick cases and on the caps of pens. Decorative clocks, mini clocks, clocks in brooches, and pendant clocks are also exhibited. The Oris Exhibit Hall offers traveling shows that some-how relate to timepieces. While I was there, the exhibit was on jazz, with the watches of a few famous musicians on display. Definitely a worthwhile stop for people who value their time.

If you have a few hundred (or thousand) dollars to spare, very nice watches are sold in the multilevel store itself. Consider it a fine souvenir!

UPPER

MANHATTAN

EAST

CORNING GALLERY AT STEUBEN GLASS

Address: 667 Madison Avenue

Phone: 800.STEUBEN

Directions: N, R, W, 4, 5, or 6 to Lexington Avenue - 59th Street; N, R, or W to 5th Avenue - 59th Street

This little museum on the lower level of the hoity-toity Steuben Glass store is an offshoot of the excellent Corning Museum of Glass in western New York state. The gallery presents three to four different exhibits per year. With its sleek wood floors, high-quality lighting, and particularly informative and descriptive signage, it is better curated than many of the other museums I have visited. Soft jazz music played as my friend Des and I learned the history and various cultural traditions of sculpting glass animals around the world from ancient times to today.

I would be remiss not to note that the Corning Gallery has the nicest public bathroom I have ever used in New York City. The woman's room is not only spotless, but classy with iridescent green-and-blue mosaic tiled floor and walls. The colors contrast beautifully with the black stalls and extra-wide white sinks. Even if you don't like glass, stop in here for a bathroom break when you're in the area.

Upstairs, Steuben Glass sells gorgeous glass sculptures. Those who can afford it will be rewarded with their own museum-quality souvenirs.

MT. VERNON HOTEL MUSEUM & GARDEN

Address: 421 E. 61st Street

Phone: 212.838.6878

Directions: N, R, W, 4, 5, or 6 to Lexington Avenue - 59th
Street; F to Lexington Avenue - 63rd Street

Other details at: www.mvhm.org

Hidden next to FDR Drive, surrounded by skyscrapers and in the shadow of the 59th Street bridge, the Mt. Vernon Hotel Museum & Garden is one of those "I-can't-believe-this-exists" places. Formerly the carriage house for a country mansion that was built in 1799 on the site that Bed, Bath, and Beyond currently occupies down the street, the property became a "day hotel" in 1826. The museum is restored to that time period, when a trip up to 59th Street was a way to spend the day frolicking in its sixty-three acres of outdoor space and swimming in the river. The hotel served a traditional meal to the guests, who then went back to the crowded downtown environment they called home.

When I rang the doorbell, I was greeted by an enthusiastic museum staff member who took me on a tour of the museum. We began upstairs, and my guide showed me how the carriages entered the building on the second floor in its days as a carriage house. (Think ramps.) The first floor, incidentally, was a barn. Currently, the room adjacent to the carriage entryway documents the history of the property. A scale model of the green, undeveloped surrounding area in the 1800s nicely illustrates how I was standing in what was the countryside over 150 years ago.

The rest of the second floor served mainly as the day hotel's ladies' parlor room. Period furniture, along with my guide's entertaining stories, gave me a good sense of what went on here when the women came indoors from the heat and socialized. The fun involved making embroidery, listening to music, and flaunting your latest hat. Really, it was a lot of showing off your middle- to upper-middle-class status. Dances took place in the wide carpeted common area outside the parlor. Good times.

The second floor also contains the bedroom of the day hotel's only full-time guest. James Stuart, a lawyer, killed a man in a duel in England, then fled to the United States. He lived in the plain room with wood floors at the Mt. Vernon Hotel, which was not meant for overnight guests, particularly in the winter. I wasn't sure that the frozen lonely nights he endured weren't really just a different type of imprisonment. The room is recreated to look as though Stuart might return at any moment.

The first floor of the museum contains the dining room, the kitchen, and the men's tavern. The dining room table is set with a lavish meal featuring turtle soup (a favorite at the Fraunces Tavern as well) and other delicacies of day. These enormous meals were prepared in the open kitchen in the large fireplace by African-American and Irish staff. The staff may technically have been free people, but my guide noted that they operated under slave-like conditions to keep the guests happy. In the tavern, visitors can kick back and read a reproduction of an 1828 newspaper. Behind the tavern is a game room.

The garden is a peaceful and lovely place to sit and reflect. Concerts are offered on a regular schedule throughout the summer. Most interesting, if you look at the back left side of the stone building under the top window, it says "1799" in red brick. Imagine that on the steel and glass towers going up all over the City these days.

For Colonial-style items, the gift shop can't be beat. Postcards and various knickknacks are also for sale.

Finding a way to keep your pants up is a delight at **Tender Buttons** (143 E. 62nd Street, 212.758.7004), a store that is as interesting as a button museum. The walls of the long, narrow shop are covered from top to bottom with buttons. In the middle of the store, several narrow antique tables and chairs allow shoppers to examine their desired objects carefully before buying. The shop sells buttons from every era since Victorians ruled the roost with collars buttoned up to the chin to the latest trends of today. Buttons can be purchased in every conceivable material: velvet and fabric covered, wood, plastic, Lucite, metal, stone, cloisonné, ivory, and so forth. Prices range from $1,550 for a set of five silver Japanese buttons depicting samurai and geishas to 75 cents for a small, round plastic fastener. Styles range from art deco to Victorian pewter to Disney to kitsch. (Buttons shaped like toasters, anyone?) Need a small button? No problem. Some of Tender Button's wares are as small as the tip of my fingernail. Got a gaping hole to close? There are plenty of buttons as large as my fist for sale here, too. Self-service boxes of buttons slide in and out of cubbies with samples on the front. The shop also stocks trinkets such as cufflinks and small items for any vanity. Tender Buttons has been helping people button up for over four decades, and I thought the owners would be buttoned up too, but everyone at the store is welcoming and cheerful. I bought my college-age cousin a black button that said "Bitch," and the clerk and I shared a hearty laugh over it. After all, there's the perfect button for everyone here.

MUSEUM OF AMERICAN ILLUSTRATION

Address: 128 E. 63rd Street

Phone: 212.838.2560

Directions: F to Lexington Avenue - 63rd Street; N, R, W, 4,
5, 6 to Lexington Avenue - 59th Street

Other details at: www.SocietyIllustrators.org/museum/index.cms

Take a step back into the swinging 1940s and 1950s at the Society of Illustrators. The three-story townhouse has a museum on the ground floor and in the basement that offers frequently changing exhibits, but the real draw is the character of the building itself. Visitors can tromp around every day except Saturday, when the upper club floors are closed to the public. The sense of clubby, jovial camaraderie drew me in and kept my rapt attention in this offbeat gem hidden on a tree-lined street on the tony Upper East Side.

It's impossible to avoid the temptation of the staircase immediately upon entering the townhouse. Loaded with paraphernalia from Society of Illustrators' events for the past several decades, it is a trip through time. Atmosphere oozes out of stylized portraits of past Society presidents, letters, posters, and photos. I almost fell down the stairs because I was so busy studying the details of a 1963 poster for their "Girlie Show." The event was advertised as "stag only," which made me chuckle. On the second floor

landing, I absorbed a photograph of Victorian men drawing a nude male model, and imagined how shocked these
"rebels" would be at some of the later events the Society
hosted. (Or would they? You never know with those
Bohemian artist types ...)

The third floor has a club for members with a little
bar, terrace, and restaurant. I got there a bit before lunch
and wandered around the empty tables to look at their
current exhibit, illustrations from women's magazines. It's
amazing in the ways that the seven sisters of publishing
(*Good Housekeeping*, *McCall's*, *Cosmopolitan*, *Ladies'
Home Journal*, *Redbook*, *Seventeen*, and *Woman's Day*)
have changed in the last sixty years and how they have
stayed the same when it comes to depicting women in
love and in the domestic sphere. Art on display ranged
from pencil drawings to watercolors. Some works from
the late 1800s were thrown in among the more modern,
commercial pieces.

Near the bar, display cases contain letters and postcards from that most famous illustrator Norman Rock-
well, including an antiwar statement he issued during the
Vietnam War. An interesting oddity presented is a quarter
on which George Washington has been recarved into the
likeness of Arthur William Brown, a post Society president. Another display case has CF Payne's palette from
1983–2004, known as the "acrylic anvil." Hanging over
the entry to the bar are an elephantine pair of ratty canvas shoes once belonging to Wallace Morgan, who the
bartender told me was the president who obtained the

building for the Society, a palette from Howard Chandler Christy (creator of "the Christy Girl," an archetype of American womanhood at the turn of the twentieth century), and a mall stick from Haddon Sundblom (known for the Santa Claus ads he painted for Coca-Cola). The Illustrators Hall of Fame Gallery is also on the third floor.

Downstairs at the back of the building, the first floor and basement museum feature frequently changing, but always intriguing, exhibits. The works on display during my visit often were political and were done in many different mediums. From paint (oil, watercolor, tempera) to pencil, collage, and sculpture, it was all there. Some of the more intriguing works combined many styles for an in-your-face, 3-D message. Even the bathroom in the basement is stylish, papered with old exhibit posters.

There is also a museum shop with books, posters, and cards. It all made me wish I was wearing dress gloves and a hat, and smoking a cigarette from an elegant cigarette holder.

HERBERT & EILEEN BERNARD MUSEUM OF OF JUDAICA AT TEMPLE EMANU-EL

Address: 1 E. 65th Street, 2nd Floor

Phone: 212.744.1400

Directions: F to Lexington Avenue - 63rd Street; N, R, W, 4,
5, 6 to Lexington Avenue - 59th Street

Other details at: www.EmanuelNYC.org/museum.php

Temple Emanu-El is the World's Largest Reform Synagogue and the largest synagogue in the United States. As
the third oldest reform congregation in America, it is very
fitting that it has a museum that contains historical
Emanu-El items as well as general Judaica.

The security guard at the Herbert & Eileen Bernard
Museum was excited to see me. I was apparently one of
the few people who had wandered in that week. "Are you
writing a report?" he asked me anxiously when he saw me
take notes in a ragged spiral notebook. After I said yes, he
dug out a clipboard for me to use. He also opened the supply closet and searched through several boxes before tri-
umphantly producing a copy of the museum catalogue *A
Temple Treasury: The Judaica Collection of Congregation
Emanu-El of the City of New York*, which he presented to
me for free (retail value: $25).

The museum is divided into three sections. Gallery A
is the repository of artifacts from the congregation. Oil

portraits of important synagogue leaders and their wives, two of which were painted by Ulysses S. Grant's portraitist, hang here. A ginormous urn-like vase, cast in silver by Tiffany & Co., sits prominently in a display case in the middle of the room. It has an etching of the synagogue building as it stood at its previous location on Fifth Avenue and 43rd Street, as well as intricate designs of religious significance. This is the Lewis May Presentation Vase, dedicated to Lewis May, the president of the congregation from 1865–1897. The vase cost $844 to make and was presented to May at services on Thanksgiving of 1888. I found it touching, albeit hideously baroque.

Other interesting items on display include a newspaper clipping about a big wedding at the temple between Pauline Schloss and Sigmund Stonehill. The clipping both breathlessly talks up the grand event while also sneering at Jews for their pomposity. It reports that 1,000 people attended a ball in honor of the couple. A mother-of-pearl fan, lace handkerchief, and other wedding paraphernalia are also on display.

Gallery B contains changing exhibits. At the time of my visit, it was Scattered Among the Nations, a fascinating photographic exhibit about the world's most isolated Jewish communities. The communities on display were Trujillo, Peru; Maharasha State and Manipur State, India; Rusape, Zimbabwe; Sefwi Wiawso, Ghana; and Bukhara, Uzbekistan. The stories and photos of Jews in non-Western countries were transfixing. It was an amazing and extremely educational exhibit.

Finally, Gallery C is home to ceremonial Jewish objects from around the world. Many of the objects are from the Renaissance period and are beautiful. The museum signage explained everything from menorahs (Hannukah lamps) to megillat (scrolls read during the festival of Purim) to mini torahs and tzedakah (charity) boxes. Hands down, the coolest menorah is one that is shaped like a house and has a clock on it. Eight little lions stand on the porches, waiting to have their heads filled with oil, wicks sticking out like tongues to be lit.

Crazily ornate lamps hang in the middle of the room over cases displaying other objects. A "double cup for circumcision" with interlocking cups (one for wine and one to catch the blood) and a very dull looking Italian circumcision knife from the early 1700s may make male visitors cringe. Moroccan wedding items (a dress and belt, jewelry, and two fabric crowns) illustrate how diverse Jewish culture can be.

On the way out, try to stop in the sanctuary to take in the magnificent stained glass windows and ornate, colorful rafters. There is no gift shop, so you'll need to find another place if you wish to purchase a menorah or circumcision knife for your own home.

NEW YORK ACADEMY OF MEDICINE LIBRARY

Address: 1216 Fifth Avenue

Phone: 212.822.7300

＠, Directions: 6 to 103rd Street

Other details at: www.nyam.org/library

The library of the New York Academy of Medicine is a snack that temporarily satisfies my hunger for medical history museums. Located in a medieval-looking stone palazzo with carved wood ceilings and gilded walls, the library has open stacks of medical journals and books, dating from as far back as the turn of the century and covering every medical topic you could possibly want to know about. I browsed through a few while sitting at a long wooden table lit with natural light from an arched floor-to-ceiling window.

Small rotating exhibits are shown in a few display cases near the information desk and in the hall, including books, documents, medical equipment (e.g., old amputation kits from the Civil War era), and photos. The exhibits I saw on two different visits were about trephination (the ancient practice of beautifully drilling holes into the skulls of living patients), complete with screw sets and graphic illustrations, and the history of New York City's first "luxury" hospital on East End Avenue, now demolished and replaced by luxury condos. While the exhibits are confined to a few display cases, they certainly illuminated how lucky I am to live in an age of modern medicine.

Also open to the public, but requiring an advance appointment, are the library's rare book and history of medicine collections. The rare book collection is home to approximately 90 percent of the medical books printed in the United States between the late seventeenth and early nineteenth centuries. Other objects include a giant cow hairball (you can also find one of these at the Staten Island Museum, without making an appointment), "cookbooks" for herbal remedies, a framed letter from Freud, and a set of colorful illustrated pharmaceutical trading cards from the 1900s.

Sadly, there's no gift shop. Wouldn't a postcard depicting a giant cow hairball or trephinated skull be fun to send to someone you love?

M
A
N
H
A
T
T
A
N

E
A
S
T

MUSEUM OF THE CITY OF NEW YORK

Address: 1220 Fifth Avenue
Phone: 212.534.1672
⟨@⟩→ Directions: 6 to 103rd Street
Other details at: www.mcny.org

Located in East Harlem, the Museum of the City of New York is less stuffy than the more famous New York Historical Society, cataloguing the experience of the average person in New York. I find it to be the best way to get a peak into the homes, interests, and lifestyles of generations of New Yorkers.

I began my visit at the top (literally and figuratively), on the poorly ventilated fifth floor, which displays actual rooms of robber barons' former houses. Anyone who ever wondered what the Rockefeller mansion looked like in the 1880s can peer into the "dressing room's" sumptuous gold-and-green décor. The home's master bedroom, with its ruby colored cushioned chairs and sofas, low-hanging chandelier, and bed surrounded by drapery reminiscent of something in which Henry VIII may have slept, is jaw-droppingly over the top. The ceilings are painted with elaborate murals, and a niche room set behind stained glass–topped arch ways is modeled after Turkish "cozy corners."

Moving down the stairs into the commoners section, the third floor holds a toy collection that compares to that of the Forbes Galleries. The centerpiece of the toy exhibit is the Stettheimer Doll House, which was decorated over a twenty-year period by Carrie Stettheimer in a 1920s avant-garde style. The dollhouse includes art by Duchamp and other modern artists. For those into meta, a portrait of Carrie's sister with the dollhouse hangs in the dining room. A glass elevator ferries dolls up and down in the mansion. It's enough to make the Rockefeller family envious.

Other toys document more typical New York child-hoods spent playing stickball, board games, playing with Madame Alexander dolls (manufactured in Harlem), and skateboarding. The small display of historical mechanical banks, including a Tammany Hall bank ("Put a coin in his hand, and see how promptly he pockets it, and how politely he bows his thanks") and a little bank building in which the cashier comes out to collect the deposit, are especially fun.

Life-size dioramas on the second floor document the changing interiors of New Yorkers' housing from 1690–1906. From the simplicity of Dutch settlers to the lavish interiors of two mansions in Brooklyn Heights (the actual 1856 drawing room from Pierpont Place and the 1906 drawing room of the Flagler mansion, whose china collection is on display outside the Rockefeller bedroom upstairs), I got a sense of how New York interior decorating matured with the City, as well as the pecking order of the social status of wealthy families. Unfortunately, no studio apartments are included.

As befitting a museum dedicated to the City of New York, the gift shop sells all manner of New York books, postcards, and T-shirts. I contemplated buying a Victorian-style hat and hat box before realizing that I do not have the space of the Rockefellers (or even Flaglers) in which to store it.

Fishing in Manhattan? Yep, grab a pole at the **Charles A. Dana Discovery Center** (on the northeast corner of the Harlem Meer in Central Park, enter the park at 110th Street and Lenox Avenue, 212.860.1370) for catch-and-release fishing from April to October. The green and reddish-pink building seems to float over the water, perfect for the annual Halloween pumpkin parade. The Discovery Center also serves as the visitor center for the northern end of Central Park, and hosts seasonal exhibits in conjunction with other cultural institutions.

MANHATTAN EAST

NATIONAL MUSEUM OF CATHOLIC ART & HISTORY/OUR LADY OF MT. CARMEL CHURCH

Address: 443 E. 115th Street
Phone: 212.828.5209
⬆ Directions: 6 to 116th Street
Other details at: www.nmcah.org

In a tidy three-story red brick building attached to the bustling Our Lady of Mt. Carmel Church (I stopped there first to check out the elaborate shrine and interesting chandeliers that hang over the altar) resides the National Museum of Catholic Art & History. The vestibule is haunted by a sculpture created by Muriel Brunner Castanis of a "draped hollow figure devoid of face, hands, and feet." Most of the museum is given to rotating exhibits from local and up-and-coming artists, and they change frequently. The museum definitely books interesting takes on Catholicism. While I was there, the first floor galleries contained a multimedia presentation on Black Madonnas and one on modern icons.

The second floor had an unexplained permanent exhibit on objects from the Kuba Empire in Congo. Carved wooden and woven materials were on display in a small glass case in the hall. How this relates to Catholic history and art is unclear at best. One of the galleries on the second floor had a delightful collection of watercolors based on the artist's memories of growing up in East Harlem. The other gallery was empty.

Climbing to the suffocating third floor (it seems to not be air conditioned and the only other visitors on the floor scurried away quickly, complaining of the heat, as it was a blazing summer day when I visited), I was delighted to find a permanent exhibit dedicated to the history of East Harlem. Photographs documenting various ethnic groups who have called the neighborhood home over the past one hundred years are fascinating. While most of the groups (Irish, Italian, Hispanic) are traditionally Catholic, a fair amount of space is given to the community of Jews who settled in the area as well. Many pictures depict the great Italian eateries that put the area on the map, including reputed Mafia hangout Rao's (114th Street and Pleasant Avenue) and the often copied Patsy's Pizzeria (117th and First Avenue). Both eateries still serve hungry mobs of customers.

The love letter to East Harlem is rounded out with artifacts from the community. My personal favorite was the ginormous red-and-black vest worn by Nicky the Vest, the infamous bartender at Rao's. Many historical objects from Our Lady of Mt. Carmel, which has served the community since the 1880s and adapted to each new wave of Catholic immigrants, are also on display. It's obvious that this is as much a museum of East Harlem's history as it is of Catholic art and history.

The decently sized gift shop is low on wares, but what they do have is bizarre. Of course, the shop sells rosaries and other Catholic religious trinkets. Yet shoppers can also pick up Native American crafts, jewelry, and framed butterflies. For a more consistently themed browsing experience, head next door to the church, which has a large gift shop in the back. The church is fascinating anyway, with its various shrines, chandeliered main altar, and diverse groups of worshippers. Take a seat and observe the scene in respectful silence to get a real slice of New York life.

UPPER

MANHATTAN

WEST

ERTEGUN JAZZ HALL OF FAME

Address: Frederick P. Rose Hall, The Shops at Columbus Circle,
Broadway at 60th Street
Phone: 212.258.9800
Directions: A, B, C, D, or 1 to 59th Street - Columbus Circle;
N, R, Q, or W to 57th Street - 7th Avenue
Other details at: www.jalc.org/jazzED/ejhf_web/about_ejhf.html

Named for record executive Ahmet Ertegun, music aficionados and others can rejoice in the smooth atmosphere of the Ertegun Jazz Hall of Fame, located in the new Jazz at Lincoln Center complex. Sit on a leather bench and take in pictures of the various honored musicians, who flash by with accompanying pithy quotes on an eighteen-foot-long video wall comprised of twelve panel screens. Jazz, of course, plays softly in the background.

Multimedia booths and information kiosks allow visitors to learn more about the inductees. Although there are only two classes of inductees thus far (from 2004 and 2005), much is to be learned. Touch a name, and a biography and photo is projected onto a larger screen.

The hall displays a miniature version of the twenty-five-foot-tall statue of Duke Ellington and his piano lifted by nine muses that commands the corner of 110th Street and Fifth Avenue. Outside of the hall, a photo wall of musicians gives a who's who overview of jazz greats. Jazz-related items can be purchased at the Jazz at Lincoln Center gift shop.

M
A
N
H
A
T
T
A
N

W
E
S
T

NICHOLAS ROERICH MUSEUM

Address: 319 W. 107th Street

Phone: 212.864.7752

Directions: 1 to 110th Street; C to 110th Street

Other details at: www.roerich.org

The Nicholas Roerich Museum is a diverting little museum dedicated to the works of Nicholas Roerich, a Russian renaissance man who lived from Victorian times to 1947. The museum is in a fantastic brownstone right off Riverside Drive. I arrived in a pouring rain, and was disconcerted to find the door locked. However, upon ringing the doorbell, a lovely older woman let me in. (Turns out that the door is always locked for security, even when the museum is open.) As I waited for my friend Paula to arrive, the staff woman gave me a brochure on Nicholas Roerich and his life's work.

Roerich was born in Russia in 1874 and sent to an art academy after showing exceptional talent and potential. His early interest was in archeology, but he also taught art for several years in Russia. After marrying a woman of equal talent and intellect, the Roerichs embarked upon a cultural tour of Russia. Nicholas began designing costumes and sets for famous operas in the early 1900s. In 1915, the Roerichs traveled to Finland, right in time for the outbreak of World War I. After the war, they were invited to the United States by the Art Institute of Chicago, where Nicholas set up the Master School to teach all disciplines of art. In the 1920s, the family set off on an extended expedition, traveling to Tibet, Mongolia, and "Chinese Turkistan." Roerich also drafted the Roerich Pact during this time. The pact was designed to help protect cultural artifacts during times of war and peace. A banner symbolizing the pact was to be flown at all cultural institutions, showing them to be neutral bodies. The banner of peace's symbol, a red circle around three smaller red dots, is a theme throughout Roerich's work.

Over three floors, the Nicholas Roerich Museum exhibits the artist's paintings, as well as assorted other objects of Eastern origin. Most of the paintings on display are from his trips to the East, although some are scenes of Russian towns and villages. His style and the colors used are interesting, reminding me of Van Gogh. Skies swirl with color reminiscent of Cray-Pas. There are numerous paintings of the Himalayas. Others depict Eastern religious gods. The museum also presents a few portraits of Roerich as well as a bust. He looks a bit like Rasputin, with a bald head, Fu Manchu beard, and short mustache, making quite a striking figure. Signage for the paintings were in Russian and English.

After wandering around the small museum for a while, the paintings still were beautiful, but they began to feel repetitive, and Paula and I found the other objects slightly more interesting. A display case on the second floor held a selection of artifacts from the seventeenth through the nineteenth centuries, including a variety of icons, a set of elaborately painted round playing cards from Russia, and small statues of Hindu gods. There is also a very impressive bronze ceremonial hat from Mongolia with hundreds of small figures of gods covering it.

On the third floor, a huge rock is cracked in half, displaying amethysts inside. A sign explains that the geode is approximately 1.5 million years old and from Brazil. The third floor also has a computer that can be used to search art and photo archives. Pictures of the Roerich family abroad reminded me a little bit of Indiana Jones.

There is not a separate gift shop, but the lobby has prints, books, postcards, and other Roerich paraphernalia available for purchase. Everything is very reasonably priced. Overall, the museum is a nice place to spend an hour or so. Classical music lovers should also enjoy the concerts scheduled at the museum throughout the year.

CATHEDRAL OF ST. JOHN THE DIVINE

Address: 1047 Amsterdam Avenue
Phone: 212.316.7490 (general information);
212.932.7347 (tours)
Directions: 1 to 110th Street; C to 110th Street
Other details at: www.StJohnDivine.org

St. John the Divine is an unusual cathedral in many ways. Although it is the largest Gothic cathedral in the world, its architecture is actually part Romanesque. It is designed around the mystical property of the number seven and has been under construction for more than one hundred years. It is still incomplete today. (Perhaps the Longest Construction Project in New York?) Because construction is incomplete, it is one of very few cathedrals in which the nave is not shaped like a cross.

The Cathedral began construction in 1892 with plans that were Romanesque in design. However, the Episcopal congregation later decided that if they were to build a Protestant Cathedral in America to rival those in Europe, it needed to be Gothic. New plans were drawn, and in 1916 construction began on the Gothic portion of the mammoth structure.

The mystical properties of the numeral seven plays out in many ways in the building. The Cathedral is the size of two football fields plus one football, a total of 601 feet. Adding 6 + 0 + 1 totals 7, a number that repeatedly arises in Cathedral lore. The stunning stained glass rose window on the western wall of the Cathedral has ten thousand pieces of glass set into a circumference of 124 feet (1+2+4=7). The buttresses are 124 feet tall . . . you get the idea.

I learned these fascinating facts when I took the $10 Vertical Tour of the Cathedral with my husband one rainy day in January. The tour not only gives the 411 on the cathedral's history and design, it takes you far behind and above the scenes. After admiring a stone altarpiece depicting Moses, John Marshall, and Alexander Hamilton in the "law bay," our adventure began through a small unnoticeable wood side door. Flashlights were doled out to the group as we entered the very narrow, damp, and dark spiral stone staircase.

A quick ascension brought us to the triforium level, which has "secret" artists' studios. (The tightrope walker Philippe Petit had a studio there and was nearly arrested when he tried to walk across a rope he strung across the nave one night.) After admiring the view of the nave below us, we were on our way up the spiral staircase to the clerestory level, which put us eye to eye with two bizarre stained glass windows. In one window, Thomas Aquinas is depicted holding a book with a giant eye in one of the windows. (The ginormous eye is symbolic of wisdom.) A horn-headed Moses is depicted in the other. (The horns unintentionally illustrate humanity's lack of wisdom, as they emanate from a centuries old mistranslation of the

Bible indicating that Jews are horned.) These details are lost to the people on the ground, who strain their necks to merely glimpse what we saw up close.

Up and up we continued, through several doors and passages, illuminating the winding stairways with our flashlights. We stopped to admire the intricate stonework hundreds of feet above the ground, where barely anyone ever views the rosettes delicately carved on archways. The artisans continued a centuries-old tradition of saving the best work for the top, more or less for God's eyes only.

We proceeded onto the roof for a nice view of Harlem, a small glimpse of Yankee stadium, and a cool perspective on St. Luke's Hospital and its awesome clock across the street. Looking straight down is the cathedral stone yard, with huge chunks of stone ready to go into the building some day. Then we were back in the spiral staircase going up again. I could not understand how we could go higher than the roof, but that is when we entered the coolest place of all: the cathedral attic.

Who knew that cathedrals have space between their soaring ceilings and actual roofs? And that the roofs are made out of wood? (This is how fires can destroy stone cathedrals. A bolt of lightning hits the roof, which catches fire and causes the support beams to collapse.) St. John the Divine's attic happens to also hide piles of bricks that are placed on top of crossbeams above the buttresses to hold things in place. My new knowledge of cathedral engineering made me eager to be on solid ground again.

The tour ends outside on the main entryway stairs in front of the cathedral. The doorways are covered in carvings and statues, just like the great ones in Europe. (Think Notre Dame de Paris.) Be sure to look for several oddities. Under the statues of Abraham and Sara is a depiction of a lotus blossom with a baby's head emerging to represent the miraculous birth of Isaac to a woman in her nineties. On the other side of the door, beneath big statues of famous biblical figures, are small carvings showing a variety of horrible disasters that man cause. Horrid scenes of torture and pain are intricately depicted. The third carving from the center on the right is a skyscape of New York City with the World Trade Center on fire. It was designed years before 2001 to warn of the potential horrors of a bomb. Staring at the eerily prescient stone work sent chills down my spine, but it was hard to look away.

After the tour, I headed back into the Cathedral to see the chapels dedicated to various ethnic groups. All are different, but two particularly stand out thanks to the items they hold. In the St. Martin de Tours Chapel, a statue of Joan of Arc stands against a wall. Beneath Joan's feet lies a chunk of stone from the cell in which she was imprisoned in Rouen before she was burned at the stake. The Chapel of St. Columba has a silver triptych designed by Keith Haring. It depicts scenes from the life of Jesus, and was the last sculpture completed by the great artist before his death.

I then spent time strolling in the green grounds of the Cathedral. You can't miss the Peace Fountain at the front of the garden, just off the sidewalk. Take a seat on one of the leafy benches to contemplate this trippy work of art.

Celebrating the triumph of good over evil, this sculpture is so loaded with symbolism that it left me dizzy. At the base of the statue are four hand-like "flames of freedom." Twisting up between the flames is a strand representing human DNA. The double helix supports the pedestal of the statue, which is a crab. The crab represents life's origins in the sea. Balancing on the crab's shell, a moon (tranquility) faces west and a sun (joy) beams to the east. Busying up the scene further, swirls encircle the celestial signs, representing larger movements of the cosmos. Nine giraffes (supposedly the most peaceful of creatures) hang out on the crab's back as well. One of the giraffes rests his head on the chest of St. Michael, who has just chopped of Satan's head with his sword. The decapitated Satan plunges downward, his head dangling by the crab's claw. (Satan, by the way, has abs that many a body-conscious New Yorker would kill for.)

I fled from the allegorical overkill farther into the gardens and looked for the peacocks. They roam the cathedral grounds at will. I was fortunate to see the beautiful metallic-blue male as he strutted calmly to his coop late in the afternoon.

Toward the school at the back of the grounds, you'll find the Biblical garden. Only plants mentioned in the Bible or found in the Holy Land during the time of Jesus (or heartier members of the plants' genus appropriate for New York's climate) are found in this quiet retreat.

In 2001, a five-alarm fire broke out in the cathedral gift shop. Much of the damage caused by the flames, smoke, and water have since been (or are currently being) repaired. The gift shop, however, never reopened, so sadly there is nowhere on site to buy postcards depicting the Peace Fountain or other Cathedral-related items.

Need a divine dessert to complete your visit? Drop into the **Hungarian Pastry Shop** across the street (1030 Amsterdam Avenue, 212.866.4230). While nothing goes as well with tea or coffee than a triangular hamentashen cookie, the Hungarian also sells croissants, danishes, tarts, and cakes. Want rigo janci (Hungarian chocolate mousse)? They've got that, as well as dobos torte—a Hungarian nine layer cake consisting of chocolate filling and yellow cake. Hungarian has been in the neighborhood for over thirty-five years, and thus witnessed about one-third of the construction time of the Cathedral. Woody Allen fans and scandal lovers take note: A scene from Husbands and Wives was filmed here. The Village Voice "Best of 2003" found that the bathrooms here had the best political messages scrawled on the wall. With an endorsement like that, it would be a sin to pass up a stop at the Hungarian.

Browse for African wares and wears at the outdoor **Harlem Market** (52 W. 116th Street). The fancy gateway echoes the **Malcolm Shabazz Mosque** (102 W. 116th Street) down the street. The mosque is a fascinating building. Brightly colored window frames and a turquoise dome make what looks to be an otherwise squat former office-type building into a community institution.

Contemplate the mosque while sipping the super sweet Kool-Aid of the Day at **Amy Ruth's** (113 W. 116th Street, 212.280.8779), a scrumptious soul food restaurant. Owner Carl Redding learned how to cook at the elbow of his grandmother while spending summers with her in the South. From candied yams to chicken and waffles, everything at Amy Ruth's goes down easy. Comfort food at its best.

M
A
N
H
A
T
T
A
N

W
E
S
T

TRINITY CEMETERY AND MAUSOLEUM

Address: 770 Riverside Drive

Phone: 212.368.1600

Directions: 1 to 157th Street; C to 155th Street

Other details at: www.TrinityWallStreet.org/welcome/?cemetery

Trinity Cemetery and Mausoleum is the only operating cemetery in Manhattan. Although it is nondenominational, the cemetery is operated by Trinity Church, which is part of the Episcopal Diocese of New York. (Trinity Church also maintains the cemeteries at Trinity Church and St. Paul's Chapel in the Financial District.) Spread on two different plots of land on either side of Broadway, the western portion seems nicer to me. Despite the cemetery's distinction as active, there are few below-ground plots available, and they are reserved for "special citizens." The rest of us will have to make do with a spot in the mausoleum.

Like many other sites in Washington Heights, Trinity Cemetery is connected to Revolutionary War history. Although no fallen soldiers are known to be buried there, two tablets indicate where the Battle of Harlem Heights took place in 1776. The fierce battle ultimately led the fall of Fort Washington, the boundaries of which are marked a bit farther up north in Bennett Park. It is listed on the National Register of Historic Places.

Filled with beautiful carved gravestones and family crypts, many famous and high-society people from the late nineteenth and early twentieth centuries are buried at Trinity, including John Jacob Astor and naturalist John James Audubon. A more recent famous resident is Jerry Orbach, the Broadway actor known best for playing sardonic Det. Lennie Briscoe on *Law and Order* for twelve seasons. In April 2008, former New York City Mayor Ed Koch qualified as a "special citizen" when the director of the church's real estate division—a former member of the mayor's staff—arranged for him to buy a below-ground plot for $20,000. Koch will eventually be buried in what he describes as a "small mountain" overlooking Amsterdam Avenue. Although small modifications will need to be made to create a mini-Jewish cemetery (essentially, his own grave) within the cemetery's boundaries, Koch explained that it is worth it because, "The idea of leaving Manhattan permanently irritates me."

The cemetery is no Père Lachaise, but it is beautiful. Between the famous people buried there, the Revolutionary War markers, and the fact that it is the only active cemetery in Manhattan, it is worth a visit. For a special visit, a candlelight ceremony is held each Christmas at the grave of Clement Clarke Moore, author of the well-known (and often humorously revised) "A Visit from St. Nick."

MUSEUM OF ART AND ORIGINS

Address: 430 W. 162nd Street
Phone: 212.740.2001
⟨✐⟩ Directions: C to 163rd Street
Other details at: www.MuseumOfArtAndOrigins.org
❀ Appointments are required.

There is nothing I love more than museums in home-based settings. The Museum of Art and Origins is housed in curator Dr. George Nelson Preston's 1898 landmark town house. As a self-described "traditional sculpture park," the town house is a perfect setting in which to contemplate African and East Asian art. When I arrived on the stone steps, I stopped to admire the glass paneling on the huge wooden doors before I rang the bell.

Objects in the impressive collection range from late nineteenth- to twentieth-century East Asian drawings and paintings to a 3,000-year-old Egyptian mummified falcon. It also exhibits contemporary paintings by artists such as Robert DeNiro, Sr. (father of the actor Robert DeNiro, Jr.), masks and sculptures from various ethnic groups across Africa, and works from Latin American artists. The art is diverse, and whether viewing works on display in the parlor or basement, visitors are encouraged to sit down on the couch, take a book from the library, and read more about what is in front of them.

Most of the items on display belong to Dr. Preston, a former professor of art history at City University of New York, who took me around and explained many of the pieces. I know virtually nothing about African or East Asian art, and he was very patient and thorough in answering my many questions.

On the second floor, the museum hosts changing exhibitions exploring themes in African and/or East Asian art. There is also a gift shop selling clothing designed by Dr. Preston, inspired by endangered species, Asian and African traditions, and the historical surroundings of the museum. Jewelry and books are also available for purchase.

After visiting diverse cultures from other ends of the world at the Museum of Art and Origins, Dr. Preston recommends a stop at **Jumel Terrace Books** (426 W. 160th Street, 212.928.9525) for items related to the neighborhood. As uptown's only antiquarian bookshop, Jumel Terrace Books "specializes in local history and African and American Colonialist and Revolutionary books; art; and ephemera relating to the Morris/Jumel Mansion and its community, Harlem and Washington Heights. Books and art related to African America, Africa, and the Black Atlantic are our specialties." Because the stock draws on owner/private librarian Kurt Thometz's collections, appointments are necessary. The unique store is house on the garden floor of an 1891 brownstone and is one of the few shops left in New York City that permit smoking.

NATIONAL TRACK AND FIELD HALL OF FAME

Address: 216 Fort Washington Avenue
Phone: 212.923.1803
🎧, Directions: A, C, or 1 to 168th Street
Other details at: www.ArmoryTrack.com/hall_of_fame.html

The National Track and Field Hall of Fame resides in a former armory building that recently underwent an extensive renovation. The ceilings are beautifully vaulted and made of brick. However, I recommend wearing sunglasses and perhaps earplugs for your visit. Although the museum is indoors, its blinding red, orange, blue, and yellow color scheme and the sound blaring from numerous video screens assaults the senses. If the goal is to raise visitors' heart rates, it succeeds even before anyone can think about all the running, jumping, and throwing that the Hall's inductees excelled at.

After passing through the entry wall plastered with random facts about track and field (I learned it is the number-one high school sport; the fastest-growing college sport for women; and that 45 percent of marathon master runners are aged forty to ninety-plus years, so I still have time to get my act together), I headed to a corner exhibit on athletic shoes. Sneaker collectors absolutely need to see this. On display were gym shoes from 1920 constructed with canvas and rubber soles (ouch) and sprinting shoes with innovative longer spikes from 1948. The brand name companies then got into the act, manufacturing comfortable and supportive shoes. The exhibited 1963 New Balance Tracksters, gold Adidas Aztecas from 1968, 1974 Nike Waffle Trainers, and 1976 New Balance 320s illustrate the technological advances these companies brought to track and field. (Check out more snazzy and high-tech New Balance shoes that are on display in the lobby.) Famous feet graced two of the shoes on display. A pair of 1996 shoes worn (and signed by) Olympian Carl Lewis and a signed 2002 New Balance RC110 shoe worn by Khalid Khannouchi during his record-breaking London Marathon run are shown.

Gear from other track and field stars are also highlighted in an exhibit on the history of track and field. I chuckled (but also thanked goodness for Title IX) while studying photos of the 1895 Vassar Field Day, as women valiantly competed in races wearing woolen dresses. Nothing illustrates how much athletes (and people in general) have bulked up over the last eighty years than the shockingly small light-blue-and-white silk shirt and shorts worn by the 100-meter Olympic gold medalist from 1920, only one of many sweaty outfits on display. Surprisingly, the narrow shoes worn by legendary athlete Mildred (Babe) Didriksen at the 1932 Olympics (she won two gold and one silver medals) are almost twice as long as Michael Johnson's 4-ounce gold-colored shoes from 1996.

On the wide staircase leading up to the second floor, I paused to look down at the markings all over the floor below that indicated how far and long people ran, jumped, or hurled shot puts to win various world records, but I had a hard time figuring it all out. I felt more accomplished, though, as I jogged on the scale map of the New York City Marathon route, completing it in about thirty seconds. Go me! The walls surrounding the floor map display Marathon memorabilia and fun facts about the event (e.g., volunteers are ready to hand out 30,000 sponges while the Road Runners club fills 1.5 million cups with water).

The building also is home to the New Balance Track and Field Center, which offers training for runners and other field athletes, and hosts track meets. The elevated track is visible behind blue-tinted glass doors that are etched with the Hall of Fame inductees' names by year and event. Display cases also hold more track and field memorabilia. A nice touch is the list of New York City high school track record holders.

The Hall of Fame has no official gift shop, although a runner's store is open seasonally in the lobby of the Track & Field Center.

*If you must jump off a bridge, do it safely at the **playground on 174th and Fort Washington Avenue**. The park has a replica GW Bridge for kids to romp on as part of its large component piece. It looks fun.*

Fuel up with great Dominican food at **El Malecón** (4141 Broadway, 212.927.3812). Open 24/7, the restaurant serves a mix of Dominicano and gringo customers huge portions of delicious food. For breakfast, try mangu (boiled mashed plantains with fried onions and a fried egg) or yucca. Everything goes down well when chased with a batida, a fresh fruit drink. Make sure yours is made con leche (with milk).

The noisiest apartments in New York can be seen two blocks east of Broadway on 178th Street. **Four large apartment complexes** were built on platforms that float over the highway. Look down and see the notoriously bad traffic on the Cross-Bronx Expressway. Nothing like living directly above a highway to avoid noise and air pollution . . .

A tad south of 184th Street, check out the memorial marking the **site of Ft. Washington** built into the wall of Bennett Park. The fort was raised by Washington's soldiers in the summer of 1776, only to be seized just months later by the British on November 25, after the Battle of Harlem Heights took place at what is now Trinity Cemetery and Mausoleum. The Empire State Sons of the Revolution—proprietors of the delightful Fraunces Tavern Museum and some of the most random museum displays ever—erected the plaque for Ft. Washington in 1901. Although none of the original fort remains, there are other markers scattered throughout the park as well as a short wall that reminds one of the original fort's bastions.

ST. FRANCES CABRINI SHRINE

Address: 701 Fort Washington Avenue
Phone: 212.923.3536
→ Directions: A to 190th Street

St. Frances Xavier Cabrini is the first American citizen saint and the patron saint of immigrants. To see her shrine, I passed through a long dingy hallway en route to the chapel. The hallway has a display cabinet built into the wall which holds a variety of offerings left at the shrine. Most are ceramic plates, usually with handwritten messages in Spanish painted on with a gold paint pen.

The hallway also contains information about St. Frances Cabrini and the Chapel. According to the fancy calligraphy posters in the hallway leading to the chapel (with versions in English, French, Spanish, and Italian), Mother Cabrini came to the United States in the late 1800s and died in Chicago in 1917. She was brought back to New York and buried in a mausoleum within two weeks of her death. Her casket was opened in 1933 by the Roman Commission in the presence of the Apostolic Delegate. Mother Cabrini's followers were disappointed to find only a bit of shriveled and decaying skin remained on her face and hands. The rest of her remains were skeletal. The body was put back in the mausoleum for another five years.

In 1938 another Commission for Beatification exhumed her remains and beatified her. Mother Cabrini's skeleton was then covered with wax to form a body, a wax head was created for her (her original head was sent to Rome), and she was redressed in a new black gown. The rejuvenated Mother Cabrini was then placed in a crystal casket with gold trim. She was canonized in 1946.

Initially, St. Frances Xavier Cabrini was kept in the library of the Mother Cabrini High School. A chapel shrine was constructed adjacent to the high school, however, and she was later placed in the transparent alter, where she still rests today. The pulpit walls are decorated with a huge mosaic mural, depicting scenes from the life of Saint Cabrini. One scene shows Mother Cabrini kneeling before Pope Leo XIII, receiving orders to go to America. (She had hoped to do missionary work in China instead, but accepted the assignment stoically as God's will.) Another scene depicts her administering to a man in a wheelchair and a child with a broken foot. There is a (bad) depiction of the Capitol Building and the Statue of Liberty, as well as representations of semirespectable immigrants (all white, of course) dressed rather well despite their poverty.

The altar is roped off, but it is still very easy to see Saint Cabrini. She is rather short, and laid out with her hands atop her body. The body appears more than a bit waxy, which makes sense as she is essentially made out of wax at this point. As the poster in the hall reminded me, though, her wax appearance "in no way degrades from

Mother Cabrini's outstanding holiness, and in no way diminishes God's Glory . . . Mother Cabrini was raised to the honors of the altar, not because of the state of her body after death, but due to her good deeds in life."

Located at the back of the chapel is a room with a big stained glass window showing Mother Cabrini flanked by two angels. Mother Cabrini's worldly relics are displayed in a case in this room, as well as more offerings to her. The biggest portion of the display is her three nightgowns, stitched with the emblems of her convent, and several other embroidered shirts. A biretta and paten (two little cap-like things) given to Mother Cabrini by Pope Pius are displayed below her lingerie, next to a bottle of dirt taken from outside her home in Italy. On the other side of the case are her hairbrush, shoe horn, hand mirror, magnifying glass, and cane. Tons of other, mostly unexplained, little knickknacks fill the shelves. My favorite objects are a check signed by Mother Cabrini, a wooden box identified by a sign as her eyeglass case, and a spring next to a sign that reads, "spring from dentures." The spring is surprisingly huge for dentures intended for the human mouth. Those must have been very uncomfortable choppers, perhaps rivaling Washington's fake tooth on display at the Fraunces Tavern Museum.

The chapel has a great gift shop, which sells a variety of religious articles. You can buy anything from a plastic bottle of holy water to tiny fragments of black cloth that touched Mother Cabrini's body (encased in plastic, the fragments range in size starting at about a centimeter to an inch) to general plastic religious statues, rosaries, medallions, and books. I bought a postcard photo of St. Cabrini in her casket, a small fragment of cloth, and a sticker depicting a young Mother Cabrini. The woman working in the gift shop was very nice and informative. We spoke for several minutes about other saints' shrines in the United States and Europe.

Outside the Shrine gift shop is a bench labeled "Mother Cabrini's Bench." It is a nice place to rest and contemplate your visit.

DYCKMAN FARMHOUSE MUSEUM

Address: 4881 Broadway
Phone: 212.304.9422
Directions: A to 207th Street; 1 to 207th Street
Other details at: www.DyckmanFarmhouse.org

Back when upper Manhattan consisted of countryside and slavery was legal in New York, the Dyckman family operated a large farm around what is now Broadway and 204th Street. The original house was destroyed by the British during the Revolutionary War, but the plucky Dyckmans returned and built a new one in 1784. The remodeled house hovers above the hustle and bustle of Broadway on a little hill.

A little cannon hidden under a clump of foliage below a parks department sign caught my eye as I climbed up a set of stone steps into the site. (Perhaps a colonial method of deterring potential home invaders?) I walked over to the porch and knocked on the door. A young woman admitted me and gave me a quick overview of the history of the property, then let me loose to explore.

The upstairs quarters have period furniture and reflect a conversion from what was originally a sleeping loft shared by the family into separate bedrooms. On the ground floor, the two front rooms of the house are spare. One contains an exhibit about the house and its history (plus the small gift counter), the other is recreated to look like a parlor in the 1800s. At the back of the house, I was disappointed to find the relic room devoid of relics. (Everything has been removed for a cataloguing project, and the staff member told me she was unsure when objects would be displayed again.) However, the journey to the space known as the winter kitchen provides a great sense of what buildings were like before construction was standardized. Extra caution is required when climbing down the uneven steps that lead to rooms behind other rooms, until eventually the basement is reached.

During the winter, the Dyckman family's meals were prepared in the basement so that the heat used for cooking could also warm the house. The room is set up to look as it did back in the day. Near the stairs, a big rock that serves as part of the floor (it was easier to just build around it than to move it) has a "Nine Man Morris" game board carved into it by a mystery player. Nine Man Morris is a game of strategy that is played by two people. Each player has nine men. A game board has twenty-four circles in which to maneuver, although the lines in the Dyckman Farmhouse board are very faint. Much like checkers, men are moved from one space to another that is adjacent to it on the board, and the goal of the game is to capture all of your opponent's men. I pondered who might have whiled away the hours in this dark, dank basement playing, and decided that they probably suffered from enormous eye strain.

In the garden behind the house, a generation of earlier

historians thought it wise to recreate a Hessian military hut like those that dominated the hills when the British forces controlled the area in Revolutionary times. Hence, I was treated to the sight of the most insanely small log and stone cabin ever. Six to eight soldiers shared these quarters, burrowed into the slope of the hill. No wonder they lost the war.

There is a small gift counter inside, but even I barely noticed what the stock is.

 *Sometimes 400 square feet can fit the entire world, as **Scavengers of Inwood** (600 West 218th Street, 212.569.8343) proves. The charming antique/junk shop sells everything from china to notecards with black-and-white photos of the Dyckman Farmhouse to lamps to linens. Stock changes regularly, so visit often to find one-of-a-kind treasures.*

INWOOD HILL PARK

Address: 218th Street and Indian Road (Nature Center)
Phone: 212.304.2365
Directions: 1 to 215th Street; A to 207th Street
Other details at: http://www.nycgovparks.org/sub_about/parks_
divisions/urban_park_rangers/eaglecam/about_inwood_park
.html

There's a good reason I chose to live in the most populous city in the U.S., and some of it is related to my fear of the Great Outdoors, which is exactly what Inwood Hill Park is. The park offers the only natural woods, salt marsh, and bald-eagle habitat in Manhattan. Thus, it made sense to check in at the Nature Center before I set off to explore the dense woodlands that cover this park rich with Native American history. The Urban Ranger handed me a map, provided advice on trails to avoid (beware the poison ivy!), and offered some guidance to interesting sites along the trails.

Shorakkopoch is the Lenape village in which Peter Stuyvesant legendarily scored what turned out to be the best bargain in history—the purchase of Manhattan Island in 1626 for about 60 guilders ($35) in beads and trinkets. A rock marks the site of the former village, as well as the location of a tulip poplar that died in 1938, at the ripe age of 220 years old. At its largest, the tree was

165 feet high (fifteen feet taller than the World's Tallest Doric Column, the Prison Martyr's Monument in Brooklyn) and twenty feet in circumference. According to the plaque on the rock, the tree was the last living link to Manhattan's Reckgawawang people.

After paying homage to the great tree and former residents of the island, I began trekking through the woods. Some of the trails in the park were created hundreds of years ago by Native Americans and were used by early settlers as roads. Low, crumbling stone walls shadow the paths up and down the hills. As I walked on a modern paved trail, Indian Rock Shelters clung to the steep hillside slopes high above my head. A bit farther on, I passed potholes in the topography formed by glaciers. My peaceful stroll came to an end at Whale Back Rock, which looks exactly like its name.

The ranger suggested checking out Overlook Meadow, so I headed in that direction, but became a little disoriented. While she had assured me that all paths eventually lead back to a city street of some sort, panic crept around my edges. Other than a few planes that flew overhead and rustling in the underbrush from (what I hoped were) little animals, the silence was all encompassing. Before my hike, I had noticed a sign at the nature center recommending exploring the park with at least one other person, and here I foolishly was alone. While Inwood Park is safer now than it has been in years, and I clearly made it back in one piece unmolested, in retrospect, I never should have wandered off without a companion. I thought about who might be in the forest, and quickly turned back the way I came. Ten minutes later, I stood in front of a row of co-op apartments. No Overlook Meadow for me.

While there is an enormous amount to see and do in Inwood Park (in addition to the woods, the 196-acre park has baseball and soccer fields, basketball courts, marinas for boating, and picnic areas), be smart while taking advantage of the last natural wildlife refuge in Manhattan.

The wilds are sure to make one long for nourishment, so drink up and celebrate Inwood's formerly dominant culture at any of the neighborhood's many Irish pubs. As every neighborhood changes in New York, Dominicans are increasingly visible in this community north of Washington Heights. Join them for mofongo, a traditional Dominican dish of mashed plantains and pork, at **Albert's Mofongo House** (4762 Broadway, 212.567.3052). The mofongo here takes modern twists and even comes in a vegetarian variety.

THE

•

BRONX

JUDAICA MUSEUM OF THE HEBREW HOME FOR THE AGED

Address: 5961 Palisade Avenue
Phone: 718.581.1787
@, Directions: 1 to 231st Street, then Bx7 or Bx10 to
       Riverdale Avenue & W. 261st Street
Other details at: www.HebrewHome.org/museum/index.htm

Is it not perfect that a museum of old religious objects
would be housed in a retirement community with old people? Currently located on the fifth floor of a senior citizen
apartment building (although scheduled to move in the
near future to the ground floor), the Judaica Museum occupies the building's former solarium, providing one-of-a-
kind open views of the Hudson River and the cliffs of the
Palisades. The Museum itself displays a hodgepodge of
items, both religious and cultural. The small space permits
only a fraction of its 1,000-piece collection to be shown at
one time, so artifacts rotate in and out of exhibit. Like the
people living here, the objects are retired.

During my visit, I was fascinated by an exhibit featuring objects from three defunct synagogues from different
parts of the world. The closest synagogue was located in
Manhattan's Inwood neighborhood, and items shown
include personal items like kippot (skull caps) from a
1958 wedding and a 1968 bar mitzvah. Religious objects
include a miniature traveling torah used in the homes of

mourners, and German-language prayer books written in Gothic print from as long ago as 1905.

On display from a German synagogue destroyed during Kristallnacht is a torah found in the local police department's basement in the 1950s, where someone hid it for safety. It is a poignant reminder both of what was lost during the Holocaust and also that even in the darkest times there are good people in the world. A display case facing the recovered Elmshorn Torah contains a scroll originally from the Alsace region of France that found its second home in a temple in Gaza. Items known as wimples—cloth pieces made from boys' swaddling garments that are used to bind the torah—are also presented, along with pictures of the synagogue before it was abandoned.

The museum's randomly selected items on exhibit during my visit included Kiddush cups of various sizes from around the world dating from the 1800s to today, late nineteenth-century matzo rollers that reminded me of pizza cutters, a gauche silver Tiffany decanter from 1860 depicting the biblical story of the two spies who returned to the Israelite desert encampment (in this scene, the spies are bearing ginormous grapes in a person-sized bunch); and souvenirs from Israel, mostly from the 1920s, including a trove of elegant leather-and-brass prayer books among the typical ashtrays, paperweights, and other knickknacks.

My favorite items are from Italy and Spain. The Museum has a gold Italian amulet from the 1700s that was used to ward off evil spirits at the time of a baby's circumcision. The locket opens to reveal the scene of an angel intervening to save Isaac as Abraham prepares to sacrifice his only child. (If that isn't a metaphor, I don't know what is.) Another item of particular note turned out to be a forged piece. A plate holds two doll-sized cups and contains miniature Shabbat candlesticks and a menorah in hidden compartments. It is supposedly a set used by Marranos, Jews who were forced to convert to Catholicism, many of whom continued to practice their religion in secret. The idea behind the forgery was to create an object to evoke pride in Jewish perseverance in the face of adversity.

Before departing the complex, visitors should walk through the grounds to enjoy the scenic setting as well as the Hebrew Home's many sculptures scattered among the buildings. The museum has no gift shop.

While you're in the neighborhood, why not do as the locals do and grab a corned beef or pastrami sandwich from Loeser's Kosher Delicatessen (214 W. 231st Street, 718.601.6665)? In the tradition of the finest kosher delis, the cheesy wood paneling is nearly undetectable under the dozens of family photos and yellowed news clippings on display. Signs in the window and behind the counter look like they've been up since the restaurant opened in 1960 and encourage folks to "eat kosher corned beef." I took their advice and enjoyed my sandwich on the subway. They even wrapped a perfectly seasoned pickle up for me. Mmmmm . . .

EDGAR ALLAN POE COTTAGE

Address: Poe Park, East Kingsbridge Road & Grand Concourse
Phone: 718.881.8900

Directions: D to Kingsbridge Road; 4 to Kingsbridge Road
Other details at: www.BronxHistoricalSociety.org/about/poecot-
tage.html

In the middle of the bustling urban Bronx sits a tiny white
cottage built in 1812. Edgar Allan Poe lived there with his
wife Virginia and mother-in-law from 1844 until he died
in 1849. In that time, he wrote *Annabel Lee*, *Eureka*, and
The Bells. Virginia, stricken with tuberculosis, died in her
bed at the cottage in 1847. After Poe died two years later,
his mother-in-law sold most of the household posses-
sions and moved. By 1895, the cottage was in danger of
destruction as the Bronx grew and buildings sprung up
around it, forcing it back from the street. Alarmed, in
1913 the New York Shakespeare Society bought the structure and arranged for it to be moved across the street into
a park to ensure its permanency.

As Poe's mother-in-law sold most of the household
furnishings upon his death, the five-room cottage mostly
consists of furniture from the period set up to look as
though Edgar had gone out for a stroll and will return at
any moment. The kitchen table is set, and Poe's desk in
the parlor has a quill pen on it, although our tour guide

Suzanne Reisman

Suzanne Reisman

told my friend Sara and me that Virginia's coffin was displayed on it after her death. Descendants of Poe's former neighbors who bought the original furniture were kind enough to donate three items to the museum: a mirror, Poe's rocking chair, and Virginia's actual deathbed.

After peeping into the small bedroom off the parlor to see the bed, I eagerly climbed the semi-hidden, steep staircase to visit the two-room attic. Poe used one of the rooms for his study and the other one was a bedroom.

Poe's concept of an ideal room, which the Brooklyn Museum staged on his 150th birthday, hangs in the hall.

The Poe cottage could clearly use some additional funding for maintenance, so head over to the little gift shop in the kitchen. As expected, Poe's books are sold, as well as postcards depicting the cottage. In keeping with Poe's literary themes, the shop also stocks cat-shaped cookie cutters in honor of his cat, Caterina, as well as ghost erasers and pencils.

To ward off any bad vibes that may follow you from the sad Poe Cottage, head over to **Original Products** botanica (2486-88 Webster Avenue, 718.367.9589). The efficient warehouse environment is not intimidating, and the cashier told me that it is the biggest botanica in New York. Amulets, oils, rocks, religious statues, and protection from malevolence are easy to obtain. I purchased a pretty pink-and-white fifteen-ounce can of "Go Away Evil" air freshener, which harnesses the protective power of the Seven Indians, for less than three bucks.

Believed to be the largest armory in the world, no directions from Kingsbridge Avenue stations of the #4 or D trains are needed to find the **258th Field Artillery Armory** (29 W. Kingsbridge Road). The armory is a fascinating site. The outsized fantasy castlelike structure with a unique roof takes up four city blocks. The building was completed in 1917 and used by the National Guard until 1994. In 2000, the City set aside funds to turn the building into an entertainment and sports complex, but all of the money was

used to repair the roof alone. Sadly, not much seems to have taken place since then and a barbed wire fence surrounds the entire structure. Perhaps one day, people will again be able to enjoy it from the inside, but for now, stop by just so you can boast that you've been to the "World's Largest Armory."

Suzanne Reisman

HALL OF FAME FOR GREAT AMERICANS

Address: Bronx Community College Campus, University Avenue and
181st Street
Phone: 718.289.5161
🖱️ Directions: 4 to Burnside Avenue
Other details at: www.bcc.cuny.edu/hallofFame/

Billed as the "original Hall of Fame" in America, there is
much to love about the Hall of Fame for Great Americans,
starting with the idea. Back in 1900, the campus belonged
to New York University. For no discernable reason other
than that people liked grand schemes at the turn of the
century, the chancellor of NYU decided that the construction of the new undergraduate portion of the campus
should include a Hall of Fame. An open air colannade was
built behind the beautiful Gould Memorial Library
(which, as a side note, I point out would be an amazing
place for a wedding—the building's rotunda is stunning,
and how much fun would it be to have photographs made
with some of the busts in the hall of fame in the background?), with spaces for 102 busts of great Americans to
be nominated over the course of the century or so. The
Hall opened in 1901.

The colonnade is classically beautiful and serene,
overlooking the Palisades. (You definitely forget you
are in the Bronx.) There are ninety-eight Great Ameri-

cans in the Hall of Fame, at first orderly arranged by subject matter—Authors, Teachers, Scientists, Septimi (I still can't figure out what that means but it seems related to music), Soldiers, Jurists, and Statesmen—degenerating into an unorganized hodgepodge of folks by the end. An inset in the floor introduces you to the subject at hand.

Each Great American is represented by a bust sitting in a niche on a ledge; a very large plaque below sort of explains who the person is and what makes him (or rarely, her) great. The plaques are random in what they say, ranging from a snippet of poetry to a line of music to a brief biography. I can not say that I left knowing who each of these people were or why they were great since some of the plaques are on the cryptic side, but that certainly makes it different from other Halls of Fame, where they bore you to tears with details.

The busts are rather uniform in style, with the great person shown in period costume and hairstyle, with the odd exception of two: FDR and Alexander Hamilton. For some reason, FDR is just a head mounted on a stick, done in a very modern style, and Alexander Hamilton looks like an ancient Roman, as he has no costume on his bust's limited torso, only a diagonal stripe. Another slightly amusing note: The NYU motto *perstare et praestare*, to persevere and to excel, appears twice in the floor of the colonnade, lest you should forget that this wonderful creation is the brainchild of good old NYU.

Teetering on the edge of bankruptcy, NYU sold the

entire campus—Hall of Fame included—to the City of New York in 1973. Today it forms the grounds of the Bronx Community College.

There is no gift shop.

As you walk to the Hall, you will pass by a stone wall and park area rising over the sidewalk at Burnside and University Avenues, a.k.a. **Aqueduct Walk**. This is not just any park, but in fact is a small portion of the Old Croton Aqueduct Trail, which ran from the Croton Dam in Westchester to 42nd Street in Manhattan. According to the New York City Parks Department, the stone walls are remnants of the outer wall of the aqueduct itself. Built between 1839 and 1842, the Old Croton Aqueduct was the major source of clean drinking water for the City until 1959. Some claim that New York City's drinking water tastes so good because the pipes used to bring the water down from the aqueduct were not made of lead. Whether it's true or not, the park provides a nice peek into the inner workings of historic New York.

OUR LADY OF LOURDES GROTTO AT ST. LUCY'S CHURCH (A.K.A. LOURDES OF AMERICA)

Address: 833 Mace Avenue

Phone: 718.882.0710

Directions: 2 or 5 to Allerton Avenue

Until I read about Lourdes of America, I did not know that it was possible to create a site for miracles by merely building a new one in the same image as the famous one, but there it is. The American Lourdes Grotto was built at St. Lucy's Church in 1939 by Monsignor Pascale Lombardo. Since then, hundreds of people swear its running water (the same NYC tap water our sinks spit out) has cured them of various ailments, ranging from stomach aches to cancer. The church proudly posts newspaper accounts of these miracles, starting the same year the grotto opened. Perhaps this is why, on a sunny and mild Wednesday morning while I was there, people streamed in and out of the shrine and church.

The gray stone grotto is a fairly large cave-like structure, reaching a height of thirty feet. In the large niche in the grotto's middle, two tables full of blue votive candles are set up. On the high right side of the grotto, a smaller niche contains a statue of Mary, her paint peeling off. A vigorous stream of water pours down the grotto's façade. (Hopefully, it is not lead paint that is peeling off Mary, as people are drinking the water that runs by her over the stones.) People of every ethnicity and age group lined up with empty two-liter soda bottles and gallon plastic orange juice cartons to capture the blessed water and take it home with them. Most of them also cupped their hands to the water and use it to wash their faces, necks, legs, and feet. I also drank from the shrine, but sadly it did not cure my asthma or allergies.

Immediately inside the church is the Hall of Saints. Those seeking answers to their prayers can light a votive candle in front of any of the numerous statues. I entered the rectory to use the bathroom, which doubles as a janitor closet. Ironically, "Borderline" by Madonna was playing in the background from some unseen radio.

Next to the chapel is the gift shop, which sells books, rosaries, charms, statues, pictures, medallions, and amulets. I waited in line to buy an official Holy Water Lourdes of America plastic flask while a man at the counter ordered 150 medallions for his upcoming nuptials. Some miracles take more time than others.

MARITIME INDUSTRY MUSEUM AT SUNY MARITIME COLLEGE

Address: 6 Pennyfield Avenue

Phone: 718.409.7218

🚇 → Directions: 2 to E. Tremont or 6 to Westchester Square, then Bx40 bus to Ft. Schuyler (last stop)

Other details at: www.MaritimeIndustryMuseum.org

The Maritime Industry Museum may have brought me to the farthest corner of the city imaginable. After taking the subway to the bus, I traversed the SUNY Maritime College campus to arrive at Ft. Schuyler, situated under the Throggs Neck Bridge. Uniformed cadets sporting crew-cuts eyeballed me suspiciously as they marched to their classes, stopping at corners and snapping their feet together before making dramatic ninety-degree turns toward their destinations. The campus is very green and surrounded by the Long Island Sound and East River. (On a sunny mild day, it makes a lovely spot for a picnic for those who live nearby or feel like schlepping up to this most out-of-the-way spot.)

Once I arrived at the fort, I wandered aimlessly until I found the museum, which occupies the hallways of a SUNY classroom building within the massive gray stone walls of the fort. As I perused the model ships, I could hear a professor lecturing about junk bonds. The displays continued into people's offices at each end of the hallway.

Besides ogling hundreds of model ships, ranging in size from a few inches to several feet long, and covering seafaring vessels from luxury cruise liners to submarines, the museum offers plenty of items to touch. At the station labeled, "What the U-Boat Kapitan Saw—or Thought He Saw," I stuck my face into the viewer of a periscope, pressed a button that lit the display, and then turned a wheel. Toy ships rotated into my sightline.

Another interactive station with no explanatory signs seemed to place me in the shiny wood cabin of an old ship. While standing at the wheel, I discovered that I couldn't see out the portholes. This did not bode well for my future as the captain of a pirate ship, I reckoned. I fiddled with various nautical gadgets in the cabin for a few minutes before setting off to find a new adventure in the mysterious dank halls of the 150-year-old fort.

Many of the items exhibited are in unlit display cases, making them impossible to see. Even the illuminated cases contain few explanations of the artifacts inside. However, the huge collection, started in 1986 by SUNY staff, contains everything from old photos and uniforms to navigation equipment and ropes. The section on cruise ships, which displays place settings from luxury liners and posters and brochures offering fun in the sun, is especially enjoyable. Although I loathed my own experience on a modern cruise liner (too claustrophobic), I found myself seduced by the old menus and promises of relaxation. A deck chair hovered over my head on a platform, reminding me that I hate the lower decks.

The many models and recreated sea scenes delighted me. From a 1930s United States Lines captain's office to a replica 1940s cadet locker stuffed with castanets, a signed photo of a blond woman ("All my love, Shirley"), books, a camera, and a sailor cap stenciled "Gershenoff," I was tickled pink. The scale model of the Brooklyn Navy Yards as they were from 1942–1944 took eight years to build. It contains forty-six naval vessels, 273 shipyard buildings, eight piers, six dry docks, forty-seven Mobil cranes on trucks, 231 railroad freight cars, and sixteen diesel engines. Outside of the yards, the model takes into account 659 surrounding homes, eighty-six adjacent factories, and four churches.

Courtesy of SUNY Maritime Industry Museum

If all this is not enough, the museum's turret stairwells display photographs of lighthouses. The museum director passed by as I wandered around, and stopped to answer any questions I had. Consider calling ahead to arrange a tour of the two-story museum. The only thing that could have made my visit better was staff at their gift cabinet, which sold all manner of knotted key chains, books, pins of famous ships, and of course, ship models, but it was closed during my visit.

QUEENS

STEINWAY & SONS PIANO FACTORY TOUR

Address: 1 Steinway Place
Phone: 718.204.3164
Directions: N or W to Ditmars Avenue
Other details at: www.steinway.com/factory/
Reservations are required.

In my experience, there is one sure sign pointing to a good factory tour: They give you goggles at the door. The Steinway piano factory tour far exceeded my high expectations. Two guides affiliated with the Astoria-Long Island City historical society walked a large group through the factory for over two hours, demonstrating the nine-month-long piano-making process, giving free samples and making jokes about competitors' "piano-shaped objects."

As the assembled group left the conference room to begin, Debbie, one of the guides, explained why the goggles must be kept on at all times, stating, "We don't ride through the factory in boats, fancy cars, or piano crates. This is not Disney World." Thus the tour started at a hideous, olive-green upright piano from 1945. Bob, the other guide, explained that these "Victory Pianos" were manufactured during World War II. Growing federal concern over low troop morale inspired the government to ask Steinway to build pianos that could be air dropped onto battlefields so soldiers could amuse themselves during down times. The crates that the pianos were dropped in were so strong that troops sometimes used them for shelter.

Our group headed outside for a quick stop to see where the wood used to build the pianos sits outside for a year to dry out the moisture that is inherent in all cut trees. Then, we continued our visit to the birthing room, where the rim of a piano is created. As we watched, five burly men wrapped wood around a piano-shaped cast, tightening the knobs and levers of a vise as they worked. This is the same way Steinway made pianos in the 1870s.

The veneer room has the oldest working machine in the factory, a steam-powered wood cutter that is on the floor for demonstration. As the name of the room suggests, this is where the veneers are made. The veneer vault holds approximately $1 million worth of wood, all sliced to 1/32 of an inch before being sewn together in sheets and applied to the poplar core of a piano lid. Debbie and Bob surprised the group with free paper-thin pieces of East India rosewood to take home.

At different points along the tour, Bob highlighted the unique patented machinery developed by Steinway to create more efficiencies in the piano-building process. We watched a computer-programmed machine cut piano legs before moving on to the lacquer room, where I felt lightheaded from the smell of polish. (It takes eight hours to polish a piano using shellac, varnish, and lacquer. I don't know how the craftsmen can stand it.) In the art/specialty department, the foreman explained how custom-made and special-edition pianos are created.

In the oldest part of the factory, built in the 1870s, we were reminded that the facility is still not air conditioned even though electricity was added in 1892. (This was one of the first buildings in Queens to be wired for power.) Operations are shut down July and August due to the heat. The group then tromped into a modern wing, and Bob demonstrated how a piano key's mechanism works. When a musician presses a key, a felt-covered wood piece (called the hammer) strikes the wire to produce sound. Some of the material used in this part of the piano is as thin as a human hair. Bob told us that women tend to work on these parts because their fingers are more nimble, but in the good ol' days, kids were the employees who built this part. Debbie then smiled and gave us all our very own hammer reject to take home.

Everything comes together in the belly department. The guts are put into the piano case, and, not unlike in a line dance, a row of empty piano cases sat opposite a row of gold cast-iron harps, waiting to join together in harmony. It can take up to several days for a craftsman to get the perfect fit.

Our tour ended in a tuning room. A man sat at a shiny ebony piano that was propped up on a dolly because the legs had not yet been attached. He played us a private concert. I don't know very much about music, but the sound was so beautiful that my cynical eyes filled with tears under my goggles, fogging them.

Usually, the last stop on a tour is in the selection room,

a specially outfitted room in which artists come to pick their instrument. The room is designed to change the acoustics to mimic a variety of settings, so someone like Bobby Short can hear what a piano would sound like in a cabaret, whereas a concert pianist can test out the sounds of Carnegie Hall. Bob and Debbie said that a 1836 kitchen piano that Steinway built that looks more like a harpsichord than a piano is in there as well. My group missed this spot because we took too long in the other parts of the factory, and the factory closes for lunch.

There is no gift shop, but I received plenty of free souvenirs during the tour, so I'm not complaining.

The Steinway factory tour wraps up at lunchtime, and there's no better neighborhood for eating than Astoria. Within a few blocks, hungry folks can find bakeries to suit any tooth: Greek (**Victory Sweet Shop**, 2169 Steinway Street, 718.274.2087), American (**Martha's Country Bakery**, 36-21 Ditmars Boulevard, 718.545.9737), French (**Ste. Honoré Patisserie**, 33-18 Ditmars Boulevard), and Italian (**La Guli**, 29-15 Ditmars Boulevard, 718.728.5612, which also serves gelato and has been in business since 1937). Walking farther down 31st Street toward Long Island City, you can dine on perfectly seasoned souvlaki on a stick to go from **Opa! Souvlaki** (28-44 31st Street, 718.728.3638), a neighborhood institution since 1969. Fresh Greek artisanal breads and Greek doughnuts are available at **Yaya's Bakery** (28-46 31st Street, 718.932.3113).

SOCRATES SCULPTURE PARK

Address: Intersection of Broadway and Vernon Boulevard
Phone: 718.956.1819
@→ Directions: N or W to Broadway
Other details at: www.SocratesSculpturePark.org

Socrates Sculpture Park was an abandoned riverside
landfill and illegal dumpsite until 1986, when a coalition
of artists and community members turned it into an
open studio, exhibit space, and public park. The charm of
Socrates Sculpture Park lies solely in the little stone wall
that encircles it. The wall is made of stone odds and ends
that look like they could have come from building
facades, streets, and who knows what. Some stones, however, are sculpted to look like children's alphabet blocks.
"BEAR OTTO" is spelled out at one point. I have no idea
what that means, but it is very cute.

Inside the park, which is jointly maintained by the
New York City Parks Department and the Pratt Institute,
are some very odd sculptures. Exhibits change frequently. During a visit, my friend Steph and I doubted
whether a flagpole with a flag hanging on it counted as a
sculpture, but it had a little sign crediting the artist and
explaining the piece, so what do we know? Other sculptures displayed at the time of our visit included a 1/10
scale model of Old Faithful that erupts every 30 minutes

when triggered via the Internet, a giant 8-foot cube made of "topsoil and endlight fiber," a 21-foot-tall reproduction of an oil rig, and a 20-foot-tall 2-D aluminum Jolly Green Giant.

Being a city park, people freely ignored the signs to not walk on Old Faithful. We kept waiting for an eruption to blow someone in the air, but were disappointed. (Perhaps the Internet was down?) In a secluded corner of the park near the water, a man stood masturbating (or possibly shaking off after urinating) in the bushes. I am fairly sure this was not a performance art piece, as the park's other visitors were assiduously ignoring him.

Socrates Sculpture Park is the only place in New York City "specifically dedicated to providing artists with opportunities to create and exhibit large-scale work in a unique environment that encourages strong interaction between artists, artworks, and the public," and all sorts of fascinating work is happening on the periphery. (I still don't think that explains the "performance artist," though.)

At the back of the park, behind barbed-wire fence and a menacing, rusted "Beware of Dog" sign, intriguing giant metal sculptures are tantalizingly out of reach, surrounded by bulldozers and other construction equipment and debris. Metalwork of some sort could be heard going on in a rusty shed. Outside the fenced-off area, storage sheds hold huge power tools and the sounds of woodworking could be heard. A lovely staircase was being built for some purpose (a construction site elsewhere, perhaps?) and there were huge wood platforms. In a shanty, families were doing arts and crafts projects.

Feel free to bring the kids, although I recommend keeping them away from the bushes. Sadly, there is no gift shop.

*Trying to understand the sculptures in the Socrates Sculpture Garden can sure make you thirsty, so head over to the **Bohemian Hall and Beer Garden** (29-19 24th Avenue, 718.274.4925) for some pitchers of delicious Czech beer. Better yet, greasy helpings of pierogies and Kielbasa can restore puzzled brain cells and soothe the soul. Construction on Bohemian Hall began in 1910 by the Bohemian Citizens' Benevolent Society to serve as a gathering place for the Czechs and Slovaks who came to New York and settled in Astoria. It is sadly the last remaining Czech and Slovak beer garden in the City. Free Czech classes are offered on Friday nights for children ages 6 to 13, giving the kids something educational to do while you chug. Fun for the whole family!*

5 POINTZ

Address: Davis Street off Jackson Avenue

E-mail: meresone@aol.com

Directions: 7 to 45th Road Court House Square;
E or V to 23rd Street/Ely Avenue

People sometimes refer to architecturally stunning buildings as works of art. Five Pointz means this literally. The warehouse serves as a canvas for graffiti art. Just because the building is bombed with graffiti does not mean this is not a curated exhibit of sorts. Before putting paint to the walls, artists must apply for a permit and create their masterpieces during regularly posted hours.

The results are awe-inspiring. Get the best overview of the building from the 7 train as it rounds a curve between the Hunts Point and 45th Road/Court House Square stations. From the ground, the details boggle the mind. I started at the Crane Street side of the structure that occupies a full city block. Vibrant pictures in pink, yellow, blue, and green dominate. Towards the rear by the train tracks, the one-story garage doors are covered from roof to sidewalk (including the sidewalk) in day-glo paint that practically pulsates. (I was also nearly overcome by the aroma of fresh donuts, which I assume emanated from the unmarked factory next door.)

The Davis Street façade, though, is where the action

is. Small groups of young men hung around the site, taking pictures and talking about their work. Murals dominate. There's an aqua underwater scene of divers swimming with manatees and dolphins. Across the courtyard, surly-looking Simpsonesque characters create mischief. Inside, near the shabby office, a set of doors on a cargo elevator wield a sinister Joker-ish face. Even the Dumpsters are covered with graffiti. I cracked up when I saw a bent over butt with turds coming out gracing the side of a trash bin. (Keep in mind that this is a living museum of sorts, so the art changes.)

Supposedly, it is possible to go up to the roof to check out the art up there as well as bask in an unobstructed view of the Manhattan skyline, but the office was closed when I got there and I didn't see anyone to ask. E-mail graffiti master Meresone for more information if you want to try to get up there.

LOUIS ARMSTRONG HOUSE

Address: 34–56 107th Street
Phone: 718.478.8274
✎➤ Directions: 7 to 103rd Street - Corona Plaza
Other details at: www.satchmo.net

Many things about the Louis Armstrong House amazed me. Currently, it is the only jazz musician's house open to the public. The house is also a testament to the humbleness of Louis Armstrong and his wife Lucille. As one of the most famous musicians of his time, Armstrong had considerable wealth, and yet he chose to live in a simple red brick house in a middle-class neighborhood in Queens. The house was sold to them by their neighbor and family friend, Selma, who still lives next door. (I was lucky to meet Selma as my tour ended.) When they moved into the house in 1943, the Armstrongs were only the second black family to live in the area.

The Armstrongs' house was originally designed as two separate flats. Lucille's mother lived in the second-story apartment, and Lucille and Louis crammed into the tiny one-bedroom unit on the ground floor. Their bed took up the entire bedroom. After Armstrong's mother-in-law passed away, Lucille renovated the building into the structure you can tour today. The fine decorations show Lucille's excellent taste, but it is still, by most standards, a modest-sized home. As I toured the house, I repeatedly compared it to the mansions and estates shown on *MTV Cribs*, and laughed.

Tours of the house begin in the living room, which has a very Upper East Side stylish feel, circa a previous era. The furnishings reflect the extensive travels of the Armstrongs. The hand-carved window shutters are from Morocco. A Baccarat crystal chandelier provides light. Ceramics and other knickknacks from around the world line the shelves. I particularly loved Louis's collection of five, strange, square matchbooks with olden-days drawings of animals on them, and his set of art deco cigarette lighters. For entertainment, the Armstrongs and guests relaxed in front of a "modern" 12-inch color TV set encased in a giant wood cabinet manufactured in 1963.

The living room is also the place where I learned Funny Fact #1 about Louis Armstrong: He liked to audio record everything that went on in the house, from conversations during parties to him just sitting around telling it like it was. The tour guide pressed a button in the wall, and I was treated to the sound of Louis's semi-intelligible thoughts during a party. While the recordings serve as an unusual way to access a dead icon, they also creeped me out just a little.

My tour guide and I moved down the hall. Lucille covered the first floor with special sea grass wallpaper, including the interior of the hallway utility closet. (Now that's luxury!) The first-floor bathroom is more similar to the extravagant homes we expect of famous musicians.

The fixtures are 24-karat gold, and the marble sink's faucet is shaped like a swan with swan neck handles. Although the gilt room is covered in marble and mirrors, it doesn't fully disguise its tiny size. The Armstrongs may have decorated their house like the Rockefeller mansion, but at the end of the day, the couple lived in a fairly small space.

Both the dining room and kitchen reveal Lucille's decorating ingenuity. As the dining room is done in an Asian motif, complete with bamboo curtains, it would not do to have a large air conditioning unit creating an eyesore. Lucille arranged for a custom cabinet to be built around the machine, hiding it behind screens.

Immediately upon stepping foot into the highly specialized kitchen, I knew that if I ever remodel the small kitchen in my own apartment, I would recreate this one. The mini teal kitchen utilizes every square inch of surface area. Designed in the 1960s, cabinets line the wall from floor to ceiling, and hidden compartments reveal built-in appliances, like an electric can opener on the wall and special slots to slide a mixer or blender right into the counter. Other spots function like secret passageways. Push a panel on the counter, and a paper towel or a plastic wrap dispenser pops up. Even the size of the stove is unique to make it fit into a narrow space. It has a plaque noting that it was custom made for Mr. and Mrs. Armstrong.

Tromping back to the front of the house, my guide and I paused at the stairs. Armstrong installed a brown leather chair lift back in 1971. I chuckled when I was told that he delighted in giving neighborhood kids rides up and down the stairs. However, it did make the remaining stairway rather narrow, so I climbed up carefully to the second floor.

The upstairs space is also limited, but elaborately decorated. The master bedroom is covered in silver foil wallpaper. The blinds continue the wallpaper pattern when they're closed. At the front of the room across from the bed is a prayer nook, and a small TV sits on a recessed shelf. The A/C is secreted behind a filigree screen. Many of Mrs. Armstrong's personal items are on display, including a freaky clown doll arranged on a little sofa in the prayer nook. Lucille's nightgown is laid out on the bed, and her glasses, with a case that looks like a modern cell phone holder, sit on the dressing table beside a pair of gloves.

In the master bath, twelve medicine cabinets are built into the silver foiled wall. The shower is diamond-shaped. Speakers piped in music so that Armstrong could relax while using the facilities. The bathroom is the site where Funny Fact #2 about Louis Armstrong is revealed: The man was addicted to laxatives. My guide confessed that Armstrong was also a pot head, but so are many musicians, although I suspect none of the others snookered Richard Nixon into carrying an instrument case loaded with marijuana through Paris airport security. He spent hours on the throne, and was the spokesman for Swiss Krissly laxatives. (Now is a good time to mention the gift shop sells some unusual items....)

The final room on the tour is Armstrong's wood paneled office. An old-school rotary phone sits on an enormous wood desk. Custom-made stereo equipment is built into the walls, as is a bar. Armstrong's liquors still fill the shelves. On another shelf rests a giant gold cigarette lighter shaped like a car. This is the room in which Armstrong kept his reels of recordings, both musical and personal. Copies of his handwritten catalog grace the desk. On a wall hangs a portrait of Armstrong painted by crooner Tony Bennett. The feel is definitely "man's retreat."

After the forty-minute tour, I spent some time in the visitor center that currently occupies Armstrong's garage. (A new one is planned to open in a few years across the street.) The center houses a variety of artifacts, from photo collages that Armstrong liked to craft in his free time to his trumpet to a pile of lip balm containers from his lifetime supply of German-made "Louis Armstrong Lip Salve."

On a more serious note, several displays explain Armstrong's role in the Civil Rights Movement. Generally quiet about the injustice he saw and experienced, Armstrong was outraged at the lack of protection afforded the nine black Little Rock students who integrated the Little Rock high school in 1957. The telegram he sent to President Eisenhower expressing his disgust is on display. As the Civil Rights Movement progressed, Armstrong may not have been at the forefront, but he followed events closely. He told a newspaper that white segregationists in Alabama "would even beat Jesus if he was black and marching along." All of this led the FBI to open a file on Armstrong, several censored pages of which are presented.

In the gift shop, I bought a magnet depicting Armstrong sitting on the toilet and shilling for Swiss Krissly. The wide variety of items for sale includes stickers, CDs, books, T-shirts, and packages of rice and beans, Armstrong's favorite food.

Courtesy of Lisa Kahane, Louis Armstrong House Museum

"While you're in Queens, you have to go to this amazing botanica!" a colleague told me. "It's called **El Indio Amazonico** (86-26 Roosevelt Avenue, 718.779.9391 and 88-05 Roosevelt Avenue, 718.478.6755), and it is something else." Can anyone resist such a description? I headed over there on my way back from Louis Armstrong's house. Statues of Native Americans were the only ones who greeted me at 88-05 storefront. I was so transfixed by the array of talismans and potions for love, luck, and money that I didn't notice the chicken feet painted red, green, or black on strings of beads that hung from the ceiling until one tangled itself in my hair. In one corner, an abandoned set of crutches was propped against a wall. I assumed that the owner left them behind after being miraculously healed by the mystic El Indio Amazonico, who was not there when I visited. Another corner had a wheel of fortune. The waiting room for tarot card readings and psychic consultations at the back of the shop was full. Candles, floor wash, dream catchers, and anything else one might need to ward off the evil are sold here. As I left for the other store down the block, I tried not to look into the bloody eyes of a St. Jerome statue, and instead wound up staring at a picture of a crucified Jesus whose eyes popped open as the picture rotated. . . . At the 86-26 location, photos of El Indio Amazonico in action, healing the ill in a variety of settings including a pyramid structure and at a street fair, graced the windows. The shop sold more of the same items, and I picked up a good luck candle for $15.

QUEENS MUSEUM OF ART

Address: New York City Building, Flushing Meadows Corona Park
Phone: 718.592.9700
📞→ Directions: 7 to 111th Street or Willets Point/
   Shea Stadium
Other details at: www.QueensMuseum.org

Regardless of which subway stop you use, getting to the Queens Museum of Art requires a hike through Flushing Meadows Corona Park. The park is chock-full of interesting leftovers from the 1964 World's Fair, which as the Museum points out, was mostly staged as an excuse for New York City Parks Commissioner Robert Moses to finally build his dream park. The museum itself is housed in a building constructed for the 1939 World's Fair, Moses' first attempt to create the park, which was thwarted by the Great Depression. The park is also home to Arthur Ashe Stadium, host of the US Open tennis tournament.

The legendary Panorama of the City of New York is the main reason to head out to the museum. Created by the ubiquitous and tenacious Moses for the 1964 World's Fair, the Panorama was the largest scale model of its time. Not just meant for show, Moses intended to use the model after the Fair as an urban planning tool. It took one hundred workers three years to complete the 273 separate Formica flakeboard sections that comprise the model. All five boroughs and the waterfronts are included.

The model is so large that World's Fair attendees viewed it from a simulated helicopter ride that ran along the perimeter of the exhibit. The exhibit spans 9,335 square feet and includes 895,000 individual structures built at a scale of 1:1200. (Meaning: one inch equals one hundred feet, making the Empire State Building fifteen inches tall.) Buildings are color coded or have lights to denote function, such as a police department, or annoyingly, public housing, whose buildings are a stigmatizing red. (While I find it offensive that public housing was designed to stand out from private apartments on the model, it is interesting to see just how much of it there is in the City. It made me proud that New York is so committed to maintaining affordable housing options for low-income families.) I easily located my own apartment building as I walked around the model.

In 1992, the Panorama received a facelift of 60,000 edits intended to bring it up to date. However, the model city is far behind the enormous construction boom that has been underway in the City for the last decade or so. For example, Battery Park City is barely built on the model. Also, towering over their skyscraper neighbors, the Twin Towers dominate the lower Manhattan skyline.

As I meandered on the ramps surrounding the Panorama, I nearly fell over Staten Island—it extends under a glass portion of the floor—when the room went dark. At first I thought the power went out, but it turns out that the lights in the room adjust on a schedule to illustrate what the City looks like at different times of the day. A recorded show began, using spotlights to highlight various parts of the model while facts about the City were intoned. The show is hilariously cheesy at times, such as when Times Square is bathed in pulsating multicolored lights to illustrate its vibrancy. The recorded voice reminded me of all of New York's superlatives: Queens is the most ethnically diverse county in the country; Central Park is the most viewed park in the United States. *Yes, I am lucky to live here*, I thought when the lights came back on and I safely exited the exhibit.

In addition to the fabulous Panorama, the Queens Museum of Art has several worthwhile permanent exhibits scattered between changing shows of funky modern sculptures, large scale installations, paintings, and drawings. The Neustadt Collection of Tiffany Art offers rotating displays of Tiffany works from the home of Dr. Egon and Hildegard Neustadt, who obsessively collected Tiffany lamps starting in 1935. During my visit, two large stained glass windows were on display. One depicts an angel and the other a trellis with peonies. Other items shown include lamps of different sizes (of course); examples of types of Tiffany glass, lit from the back so they glowed warmly; and glass tiles. The Tiffany Studios and Furnaces were located in Corona, and the Queens Museum appropriately plays up this connection through vintage photos of craftsmen/women hard at work.

Given the location of the museum, it would be a travesty if there was nothing about the two World's Fairs held on the site. However, a confusingly curated ground floor exhibit has everything I wanted to know and more about both events. Oodles of souvenirs and objects from the 1939–40 and 1964–65 Fairs are on display. The premise of the first of these World's Fairs was that it would commemorate the 150th anniversary of George Washington's inauguration, so many of the items exploit our first president's image. (Is a mug shaped like Washington's head really necessary?) Items from the subsequent World Fair include one of the "helicopter" cabins that traveled around the Panorama. I climbed in and tried to imagine what it would be like floating over the model instead of gazing into an empty rectangular room through the window.

The gift shop is delightfully random. Need a Mexican wrestling mask or Day of the Dead shadowbox? You're in luck! Surrounded by the typical "I ❤ NY" crap trinkets are high-end pottery and glass, bags and purses, lipstick cases, postcards, statues of Hindi gods, and ethnic dolls. The shop also sells vintage souvenirs from the 1964 World's Fair.

Courtesy of Queens Museum of Art

POPPENHUSEN INSTITUTE

Address: 114–04 14th Road

Phone: 718.358.0067

Directions: 7 to Flushing - Main Street, then Q65 to 110th
Street and 14th Road

Other details at: www.PoppenhusenInstitute.org

The most important thing to know before setting out for
the Poppenhusen Institute is that it is essentially a settlement house that happens to be in a very funky historic
building. This was one of the places where I stupidly
showed up (with my friend Oliver in tow) without calling
first, only to find that while the building is usually open on
Fridays, the executive director happened to take the day
off. Noting my despair, the building caretaker agreed to
show us around, and did an excellent job answering our
questions.

Since the building was officially closed, we went in
through a side entrance, thus beginning our tour in the
room that housed the first free kindergarten in the United
States. One side of the room still has the original slates on
the wall and desks from 1870, when humanist industrial-
ist Conrad Poppenhusen set the classroom up just like in
his native Germany. The other side of the room holds
photos of firemen in 1800s from the Queens Historical
Society's exhibit on the history of firefighting in Queens.

When the Poppenhusen Institute opened its doors in 1868, it truly served as a multipurpose community facility for the fledgling town of College Point. As such, it housed the local jail. Two long narrow cells, painted white, still exist, located just down the hall from the kindergarten. It looked cramped for more than one person, but the caretaker told us that each cell was used for up to fourteen people back in the day. At the time of our visit, the only prisoner was a stray dog that the caretaker's family had found tied to a fence and agreed to foster until a permanent home could be found. He seemed happy enough to be there.

The basement also housed a rifle range where soldiers trained before they were shipped off to fight in World War II. Women were instructed in the art of riveting in the space, albeit not at the same time as the men. The space currently holds the archives for the property.

Upstairs, the caretaker explained that the Institute is a perfectly maintained Mansard-style mansion that was placed on the National Register of Historic Places in 1973. The halls are decorated in a very homey and welcoming manner, as befitting a community center. In its past life, the second floor provided rooms for the Justice of the Peace, a court, the first location for the College Point Savings Bank, and the first public library in the area.

There is a small exhibit on the neighborhood's residents throughout American history, starting with Native Americans. In the Matinecock Indian exhibit, a life-size diorama displays a scene from traditional Matinecock life, and children can climb into a wigwam. Photographs depict College Point in the 1800s through the present day, and most important, document historic properties that were lost due to real estate development. I appreciated the message about the importance of neighborhood preservation.

Another exhibit at Poppenhusen is the 9/11 Memorial Room. Upon entering the room, it was impossible to miss a glittery cardboard skyline with the World Trade Center majestically soaring above the other buildings in gold. The Institute displays a girder from the site, as well as clippings about people, particularly firemen, who died that tragic day. Part of the room is set up theater-style, and the caretaker played a video, rife with historic re-enactments, about the life of Conrad Poppenhusen and the Institute, which he built as a gift to himself on the occasion of his fiftieth birthday.

While the Institute has no gift shop, it does offer classes for children and adults and the third-floor ballroom can be rented for special occasions.

THE LIVING MUSEUM AT CREEDMOOR PSYCHIATRIC CENTER

Address: 80–45 Winchester Boulevard, Building 75
Phone: 718.264.3490
Directions: E or F to Kew Gardens/Union Turnpike, then Q46
to Winchester Boulevard
Appointments are required.

The Living Museum is without a doubt the most moving and socially important of all of the places that I visited while researching this book. Serving mentally ill individuals affiliated with Creedmoor Psychiatric Center, the largest of five state mental institutions in New York City, this working studio museum does not provide art therapy in the traditional sense. Rather, it is a haven for the mentally ill to create art in a protected environment.

I admit that I had trepidations when I arrived on the Creedmoor campus and found the lunatics running the asylum, so to speak. As I headed toward Building 75, I passed a group of people waiting for a bus.

"Whatcha doin' here, pretty girl?" a frail African-American woman with silver hair yelled out.

"I'm here for the museum," I replied, eyeing everyone around me nervously.

A young man approached me. "I'll go ahead and let them know you are here," he informed me and nodded solemnly before running toward the museum. I followed him, wondering what the hell I was getting myself into.

The outside of Building 75 reminded me of a summer resort lodge. The sidewalks are covered by a long overhang, creating a porchlike space, and people sat on benches smoking. I took a deep breath and walked by them, feeling their stares. When I entered the museum, I couldn't tell who was in charge. A group of people gathered around a bespectacled man with long, thinning white hair. Some of them looked up when I entered the room; others paid no attention to my intrusion.

After introducing myself and meeting the program director, a patient/artist named John volunteered to give me a tour of the museum. The museum occupies a former cafeteria and kitchen, used in the 1920s, but long deserted when The Living Museum was founded in 1983. The two-story kitchen's skylight provides ample natural light for the artists, and the maze of dozens of spacious surrounding rooms offers work space for the one hundred or so patients who create and exhibit art within these walls. On the second floor, a balcony provides an overhead view of the work going on in the kitchen area around the metallic firehoods above what was once an industrial stove. Murals, framed paintings, sculptures, and photographs cover the once decrepit walls, beams, and floors throughout the entire building.

My tour began with John's studio. His work included lushly colored primitive prints that made me think of Aztecs, self-portraits, and pornography, such as an apron with a picture of a gaping vulva over the crotch area. We moved on to another artist's studio space. Issa, another artist, paints expansive works exploring issues of race and discrimination, including an incredible mural of Dr. Martin Luther King, Jr.'s 1963 march on Washington. Issa is also interested in superheroes and has some neat paintings of them.

Upstairs, a room contains small trees and leafy potted plants outlining a path with assorted works of art created from found objects all around it. John stopped in a room with a coffee table and sofa that is painted in a way that reminds me of Keith Haring's work. "This is where we come to sleep and sometimes have sex," he told me without emotion. I silently resolved not to touch anything for the rest of my visit.

Other rooms and hallways are filled with large paintings, sculptures, and multimedia installations that explore politics, pop culture, and religion. A mural John created in response to 9/11 was featured on the cover of a Queens newspaper. One dark room (the windows are painted black) exhibits dozens of TVs with painted screens. When John plugged the work in, bizarre images lit up the space. A corner room features various religious works, dominated by angels, but also including paintings of Hindu goddesses.

John explained who created each work and the artist's intended message. After the tour, I spoke with the Museum's director, Dr. Janos Marton. Patient/artists constantly dropped by the desk, asking for his advice on their work or telling him just why they didn't want salad that day. The daily salad is made from vegetables grown in the organic garden on the side of the building, and Dr. Marton encourages residents to eat as healthfully as possible to balance out their medications. When a petite woman with brown hair offered me a fresh salad, I accepted it. It was delicious, and only after I ate half of it did I worry that I might have taken someone's lunch.

Of course, not all of the artists are masters. Several pieces are amateurish, but that is not the point of the museum, and all work is treated with respect. Many of the artists at The Living Museum sell their work, but for a pittance of what they would likely receive if they were not mentally ill, which saddens me. I left the museum feeling fortunate for what I have and glad to have met these artists.

QUEENS COUNTY FARM MUSEUM

Address: 73–50 Little Neck Parkway

Phone: 718.347.3276 (FARM)

Directions: E or F to Kew Gardens/Union Turnpike, then Q46
to Little Neck Parkway

Other details at: www.QueensFarm.org

The Queens County Farm Museum possesses many dis-
tinctions. It is the oldest continually farmed site in New
York State, dating back to 1697. Although only forty-seven
acres remain, the farm is New York City's largest remaining tract of undisturbed farmland. While other food production occurs throughout the five boroughs in
community gardens or lucky New Yorker's backyards, the
Queens County Farm Museum is the only operating *historical* farm in the city. The farm left private hands in
1926 when it was sold to Creedmoor Psychiatric Center,
which operated it as a model for the use of farming as
therapy (a.k.a. forced labor) until 1960. Visitors are welcome year-round.

To get a good sense of traditional farm life, my husband and I stopped first at the Adriance farmhouse. Tours
are available only on weekends and on a schedule set by
the tour guide, who also drives the tractor providing hay
rides. As we approached the farmhouse porch, the white-
haired ponytailed guide's Yorkshire terrier yipped at us.

The guide ignored the noisy beast and said to go on in. Several people and the yapping dog followed, and we assembled in the kitchen to learn about life in the house in the late 1700s through 1850s. The dog hung around for the entire tour, barking intermittently.

Built in 1772, the farmhouse originally had only three rooms. The kitchen contains the original floors, beamed ceilings, fireplace, and door. (The original coat of paint is even visible on the back of the door in another room.) Flowers and herbs hung upside down to dry from a string across the room. The guide demonstrated how the kitchen cookware worked, picking up semi-familiar look-ing objects and asking the kids in the audience to guess the purpose of each instrument. Through this method, we were introduced to a toe-toaster (a rotating metal rack in which bread was placed, then nudged around the fire with one's toe to brown each side); a mold that could make twenty-four candles at once; a wooden block mold that shaped a pound of butter into a rectangular brick; and a wooden shoulder harness that allowed people to haul two dangling buckets of water.

On the other side of the kitchen, a wall was removed between a small bedroom and larger common space to allow the museum to accommodate groups. The guide gave a demonstration of the swinging split Dutch door (occupants could open the top portion to let in the fresh air, but could keep the bottom half shut so that animals didn't wander into the house), which leads to the garden. He explained that the fireplace is back-to-back with the one in the kitchen so that only one chimney was needed. An antique spinning wheel occupies a corner.

In 1855, the next owners of the farm added to the farmhouse, doubling it in size. They erected a dining room with a heating stove that reminded me of a 1950s TV cabinet. A second "modern" kitchen improves on the first one with a dry sink (for which water had to be brought to the basin from outside and emptied manually) and a brick fireplace with a crane that allowed cooks to swing pots out of the fire, which reduced the risk of burns. The kitchen's furnishings are all period reproductions made by the caretaker as a hobby. The parlor has a coal fireplace and tin ceiling. Outside, a replica of a 1903 steel windmill stands in the yard.

While the farm museum is not a true petting zoo, the animal residents may be fed and touched through the fence. (Green Meadow Farms, a seasonal program operating adjacent to the free farm, allows visitors to handle all of the animals, including milking a cow, for an entrance fee.) Plastic cups and decorated metal buckets of feed are sold in the gift shop and at a table near the education center. Two- and four-legged residents of the farm include enormous pigs, woolly sheep, goats, ducks, and a cow. Two hutches house at least four rabbits (they were hiding and hard for me to count), and a chicken coop circa 1930 holds over one hundred Rhode Island hens and roosters. Pea hens and other fowl roam the grounds, where they are periodically chased by laughing children. Stations with hand sanitizer dispensers are posted near the animal pens.

Throughout the year, the museum holds seasonal events and activities (most of which are on Saturdays and Sundays) worth planning your visit around. I went during the fall when the Amazing Maize Maze, a three-acre corn maze, was open. October weekends also offer a pick-your-own-pumpkin patch. Another cool program is the Eighteenth -Century Tavern Night in which diners can indulge in an authentic meal from the 1700s prepared on an open hearth using traditional recipes. The dinner takes place in November, but often is fully booked by May.

In addition to animal feed, the gift shop sells fresh produce from the farm, jams, syrup, candy sticks, and plants. Kids will want various trinkets and toys, such as sticker books or wooden whistles. Colonial items and T-shirts are also available.

BROOKLYN

CITY RELIQUARY

Address: 370 Metropolitan Avenue

Phone: 718.782.4842 (aka 718.R.U.CIVIC)

⟶ Directions: G or L to Metropolitan Avenue - Lorimer Street;
L to Bedford Avenue

Other details at: www.CityReliquary.org

Occupying a small storefront near the heart of hipster Williamsburg, City Reliquary has big aspirations. Originally just a "window museum" on the corner of Grand and Havemeyer Streets displaying New Yorkers' collections of items ranging from vintage thermostats to presidential commemorative plates, City Reliquary opened an "actual, enterable" museum in April 2006. The young museum seeks to preserve New York City's history and inspire visitors to learn more about the five boroughs.

I entered into the main museum room through a vintage turnstile donated from a neighborhood hardware store, registering me as the 40,000th (and change) person to slide through its rotating metal arms. Much of the museum is dedicated to the hard materials that make New York what it is. In the Geology of New York I was treated to a variety of core samples displaying in six-inch solid cylinders the ground that the city stands on. Looking at the marble sample from upper Manhattan, it dawned on me how the Marble Hill neighborhood derived its name. Also displayed in large quantities is the infamous black Manhattan schist, which visitors to Central Park can see jutting out of the ground throughout the park.

Rocks, plaster, and terra cotta make up the materials in an exhibit case of architectural remnants from various buildings. The chips and chunks were collected during the repair and restoration of historic properties and donated to the Reliquary. For anyone who ever wanted to see the ceilings, roofs, or cornices from places like the Guggenheim, Flat Iron Building, Waldorf Astoria Hotel, Hearst Building, Grand Central Station, or the Plaza Hotel, here they are, up close and personal. Other interesting pieces of infrastructure come from the dome on top of City Hall and mosaic tiles from the ultra-mod TWA Terminal at JFK designed by Eero Saarinen.

My favorite exhibit in the Reliquary is a locker that opens to reveal a display dedicated to Little Egypt, the dancer who legendarily originated the "hoochee coochee" (a.k.a. belly dance) at the 1893 World's Fair in Chicago. The stage name was adopted by another exotic dancer, who became famous when she was hired to perform at a Fifth Avenue bachelor party in 1896. Rumor had it that she would dance naked, and the vice squad raided the event. Press a button in the locker, the lights go up, a window panel drops down à la peep show (homage to another part of New York City's past?), and a mannequin in a belly dance costume performs a hip-shaking dance. I found it very clever.

Next to the Little Egypt booth is a window from the original newsstand that stood at the corner of Canal and Bowery Streets for decades, named "Petrella's Point" for its stubborn owner. Items that one might find in a run-down newsstand, like comic books and handwritten signs, are on display. A gilded cage occupied by fake birds hangs over the window in homage to the bird garden in Sara Delano Roosevelt Park in Chinatown.

Lining the wall above a display case of World's Fair items (which includes a rare silent home movie in color from 1939) is a collection of glass seltzer bottles. These beauties are exactly the type of bottles that the Three Stooges might use to spray one another in the face during a slapstick moment of hilarity. Brooklyn is the former epicenter of seltzer bottling. Today, only three seltzer companies delivering bottles remain.

Rounding out the Reliquary's permanent collection is a display case loaded with Statue of Liberty souvenirs and several items dedicated to all manner of public transportation. Focusing mainly on the subway, subway maps, paper transfers, and exonumia (a fancy word for tokens, or coins of non-monetary value) are exhibited. Labeling the tokens as exonumia allows the museum to include peep show tokens from the "bad" old days of Times Square alongside the first subway tokens issued in 1953 to accommodate a 15-cent fare, and commemorative tokens, trolley tokens, and tokens for bridges. I suppose this is fitting, as some may consider visiting peep shows to be a transporting experience....

A back room holds the museum's changing exhibits, and the gift shop occupies the front of the museum. Selling an excellent variety of New York City–themed goods, the gift shop has a good sense of humor. For a mere $1, visitors can buy three "real Department of Sanitation street sweeper bristles." Plastic roaches are sold, as are pendants and earrings made from street maps, t-shirts, books, and other New York knickknacks.

Courtesy of Stef Weiss

Courtesy of City Reliquary

SHRINE CHURCH OF OUR LADY OF MT. CARMEL

Address: 275 N. 8th Street

Phone: 718.384.0223

> Directions: L to Bedford Avenue

I am Jewish, and our tradition is to bury our dead, completely intact, as quickly as possible. There's no displaying the body and no keeping any mementos. This is why Catholic relics fascinate me, although it is hard to find these pieces of or items associated with various saints on display in the United States. Much to my delight, the Shrine Church of Our Lady of Mt. Carmel—just up the street from the City Reliquary—has an actual reliquary!

The church is known for its impressive *giglio*, a hand-built, seven-story-tall papier-mâché tower that is carried on a platform and accompanied by a full brass band by Italian Catholics celebrating the feast of Our Lady of Mt. Carmel. I stopped into the church after I learned about it at the City Reliquary. The church's sanctuary is lovely, with a tiled basin containing holy water welcoming visitors as they enter. In a side chapel, the faithful can light a candle at the feet of the statues of dozens of saints.

On my way out of the church, I followed a sign for the rest room. In the left staircase in the vestibule, I was delighted to find a bust of St. Trofimena with some sort of reliquary imbedded in her chest plate. St. Trofimena was martyred at the age of thirteen, and the main trove of her relics are stored in the Basilica of St. Trofimena in the town of Minori, along Italy's Amalfi coast. I'm not sure if these relics are actually from St. Trofimena, as it was hard to read the inscription, nor do I know what they were, exactly (bone fragments?). Regardless of what is in there, it's cool to see relics right here in Brooklyn.

BROOKLYN BREWERY TOUR

Address: 79 N. 11th Street
Phone: 718.486.7422
@→ Directions: L to Bedford Avenue
Other details at: www.BrooklynBrewery.com

The only thing more amusing than a one-room museum is a one-room factory tour. Every Saturday on the hour, starting at 1:00 pm and ending at 4:00 pm, the Brooklyn Brewery "tour" takes people behind the scenes to a room where they make draft beer. On a sunny afternoon, I decided to take the plunge and see what it was all about.

While waiting for my tour to begin, I sat in the cavernous common area. The brewery is home to a happy hour on Friday evenings, and although there was no information about Saturday hours on their website, the hall was packed with people buying beer tokens and exchanging them for brew at the bar in the back. The chatty crowd was accommodated both at picnic tables and round tables with folding chairs as rock music blared over speakers in the background.

Since I'm not much of a drinker myself, I hung around the front. Three windows set into the wall display beer bottles from local breweries, all of which have disappeared. The antique bottles range from the 1800s to as late as the 1950s. Most are from breweries in Brooklyn and the Bronx, each bearing distinct logos on the otherwise smooth glass. Under some of the bottles, typed notecards indicate how many barrels a year were produced. The companies were almost universally what are referred to as microbreweries today. The display was most unexpected, and I appreciated the information.

At tour time, a perky, slim young woman gathered a hundred or so of us curious souls and led us to the promised land of beer. In single file, we tromped past pallets stacked high with white sacks of malt and empty kegs waiting to be filled. Within seconds, we reached our destination: a room filled with vat-like machines making beer all around us.

The guide clambered up a metal staircase to a platform built between two vats. She toasted, "To delicious beer!" and sipped from a clear plastic cup she brought along. I stood next to an open pit filled with an amber liquid and hoses. "Be careful," the guide cautioned as she began. "Before anyone tries to dunk their heads in there for cool, refreshing beer, let me tell you that it is filled with iodine." I took a step away from the tub. A workstation with white, plastic gallon-size jugs and foot-long glass beakers was on my left, so there was no room to move too far.

For the next twenty minutes, our guide regaled us with the history of the Brooklyn Brewery. One of the founders learned to brew beer in his hotel bathtub while working as a news correspondent in the Middle East, where alcohol is prohibited. When he returned to Brooklyn in the early 1990s, he joined up with a banker friend to open a brewery upstate and truck the brew to the City. By 1996, they were able to convert a former matzo factory into the first brewery in the City in twenty years.

The guide drank her beer, but this is one factory tour that does not end with free samples. At the end of the presentation, the group filed out of the production room and headed over to buy more beer tokens.

The counter at the front of the factory that sells beer tokens also hocks Brooklyn Brewery paraphernalia. Beer fans can stock up on Christmas ornaments, T-shirts, glasses in a variety of shapes and sizes, Frisbees, pens, caps, and even notepads in case you need to write down your thoughts lest you forget them in a fit of drunkenness.

Who says that original art is always expensive? In the garage that serves as the emporium **SKSK** (85 Wythe Avenue, www.stevekeene.com), paintings and wood figurines line the wood-trellised walls, ranging from portraits of the Beatles in Russia to roosters, spider webs, and Warholesque Budweiser cans. Sculptures of hot dogs and abstract objects, as well as wood cut-outs of people, guitars, bananas, dancers, and asterisks can also add a mod splash of color to any home. The prices are rock bottom: three small paintings for $5, and three medium paintings for $10. I bought a wooden hot dog for $3.

NEW YORK CITY TRANSIT MUSEUM

Address: corner of Boerum Place and Schermerhorn Street
(in former subway station)
Phone: 718.694.1600

Directions: 2, 3, or 4 to Borough Hall; M or R to Court
   Street; A, C, or G to Hoyt - Schermerhorn; A, C, or F to Jay
   Street - Borough Hall
Other details at: www.mta.info/mta/museum/

While I love the informative exhibit on how the subways were built, including claustrophobic pictures of sweaty men digging out tunnels, the best reason to go to the New York City Transit Museum is to go down to the former subway station tracks and poke around the subway cars. Before heading all the way down, though, check out the various tollbooths and turnstiles, and signage exhibit. (Who hasn't had the urge to steal a subway sign?) The interactive City bus is fun, too.

The trains on display rotate, so you never know which models you'll be able to explore. Boarding the vintage subway and elevated trains gave me an appreciation for the modern trains we have today. As bad as it can be now, it is hard to imagine commuting to work during New York's humid, hot summers and relying only on ceiling fans and open windows to keep from melting into pools of perspiration. (Ah, air conditioning!) Some of the "newer" cars are painted in bright blues and oranges, others are tranquil aqua. The wooden interiors and the wicker seats in the oldest subway cars are truly charming. To think that the seats actually had cushioning at one point is a depressing reflection of modern life. Some trains even have porthole windows for a truly surreal experience.

Each car has advertisements from the era. I had a good laugh/cry over the prices of groceries fifty years ago. Also of high entertainment value are the Miss Subways ads from the 1940s and '50s, featuring comely (white) lasses who won the Miss Subways beauty pageant promoting the benefits of mass transit.

Head over to the subway simulator, where you can try and "drive" a subway down a curvy tunnel. I discovered this is not a future career option for me.

The gift shop sells everything MTA and more. Shower curtains, umbrellas, and mouse pads are only a few examples of the crap emblazoned with subway maps. Cufflinks and jewelry boasting the letter or number on your favorite subway line can be purchased. Books, toy trains, and all manner of souvenirs round out the full stock options in the store.

PRISON SHIP MARTYRS MONUMENT

Address: Ft. Greene Park, bordered by DeKalb Avenue,
Cumberland Street, and Myrtle Avenue
Phone: 718.222.1461

Directions: B, Q, M, or R to DeKalb Avenue; 2, 3, or 4 to
Nevins Street; G to Fulton Street
Other details at: http://fortgreenepark.org/pages/prisonship.htm

Crowned by an eight-ton bronze urn, the Prison Ship
Martyrs Monument is the World's Tallest Doric Column at
150 feet tall. I assumed that a 150-foot-tall Doric column
would be a snap to locate in the center of Ft. Greene Park,
but what do I know? It took some traipsing around in the
leafy, hilly park before I stumbled upon the monument. I
tried to make myself feel better about the situation by
noting that it would probably be easy to find if it had not
been fenced off and blanketed by scaffolding, but the
truth is that the whole park is on a thirty-foot-high hill,
and trees hide the whole structure rather well.

Even without direct access to the monument, I could
feel its importance. Designed by the prestigious firm of
McKim, Meade, and White and unveiled in a grand ceremony in 1908, the column is dedicated to the memory of
the 11,000-plus patriots who died during the War of
Independence in conditions of filth, overcrowding, and
hunger while imprisoned on decommissioned British

ships floating in Wallabout Bay. The deceased were thrown overboard or shallowly buried in nearby salt marshes. In the years following the war, bones continually washed up onto shore. Residents gathered the remains and a crypt was built to put them to rest.

Next to the monument is the Ft. Greene Visitors Center, originally built by McKim et al. as a comfort station. Several employees sitting at information desks pointedly ignored me as I poked around. A cheesy diorama portrays the Americans burying the ship's dead underneath a sign reading, "Rebels, bring out your dead." It was wrong to giggle, but I could not help but think of a scene in a Monty Python movie. (Oh, those British!) The center also displays Revolutionary War objects found in the park over the centuries, such as a button from Wellington's coat that turned up in 2005 and some musket balls.

The park itself was designed by Frederick Law Olmstead and Calvert Vaux, the brains behind Central and Prospect Parks. It is lovely and its elevation provides awesome views of the Empire State Building and Times Square. Bring a picnic and spend the afternoon relaxing.

WATERFRONT MUSEUM

Address: 290 Conover Street at Pier 44

Phone: 718.624.4719

Directions: F to Smith & 9th Street, then B77 to Conover Street at Coffey Street; A or C to Jay Street - Borough Hall or 2, 3, or 4 to Borough Hall, then B61 to Beard Street and Van Brunt Street (last stop)

Other details at: www.WaterfrontMuseum.org

I expected the captain and proprietor of the Waterfront Museum to greet me with a cheerful, "Ahoy matey!" as I crossed the threshold of the vessel, but he was busy talking to a small group that gathered around him to hear about the history of showboat barges. As the barge rocked gently on the waves while I waited near the entrance, I realized that this is a museum that is not appropriate for people who get seasick. Quickly sinking into the nearest chair, I attempted to grow some sea legs before exploring the museum.

The Waterfront Museum is the only surviving wooden barge from New York's gloried barge trade past. Captain/curator David Sharp found it filled with muck in Hoboken in 1985. After an extensive cleaning process and some years at various ports of call, it permanently docked in Red Hook in 1994, only to be threatened by wood-eating organisms thriving in newly unpolluted waters. While the barge was dry-docked and repaired in upstate New York, the same organisms ate and destroyed the pier it had called home. Fortunately, another pier was secured nearby and the museum, which also houses the captain and his family below deck, is afloat again in Red Hook, ready to share its treasures with the general public.

The barge has many different functions. It serves as a museum of transportation and commerce, as well a space for art and entertainment in a historic setting. Regularly scheduled concerts are offered on the ship, and summer weekends include circus performances. Capt. Sharp is a former cruise ship juggler who met his partner, a fellow juggler, while working the ships. Their two daughters are trapeze artists who all perform on the barge. Tickets are sold in advance on the website and the shows often sell out.

Merely walking around the barge is amusing. While I was onboard, a lop-eared rabbit hopped around freely as Capt. Sharp shared his personal photos and news clips of a life as an entertainer at sea and shots of the barge restoration process with assorted visitors. Albums were spread out on the table near the eclectic kitchen. A row-boat and canoe dangled from the rafters along with household items and a lobster trap. The temporary exhibit on showboats hung from the walls, and chairs were set up at the front of the boat around a video about the grand old days of showboats and barges. Next to the television, a kinetic sculpture by artist George Rhodes dropped a ball into an elaborate mousetrap-like contraption, dazzling children. Old signs hung in the spaces not used for the showboat displays.

The barge can be rented for weddings and other special events. Whether learning about showboats, watching a circus performance, or getting hitched, the Waterfront Museum certainly gives ample new life to a barge that had been dumped as useless. Hopefully, one day there will be an onboard gift shop, too.

Arguably the most "heroic" store in all of New York City, the **Brooklyn Superhero Supply Co.** (372 Fifth Avenue, 718.499.9884) sells all the gear one might need to save the world, while it entertains people who pass by its curious storefront display. Need a full length cape? The Supply Co. purveys them in traditional black, green, or purple lamé, or brown velvet. Matching shiny vinyl boots are sold separately. The utilitarian metal shelving units are stocked with items like Tights in a Can, face masks, night vision binoculars, vintage utility belts that will weigh down the wimps, and x-ray glasses. Pick up air cannons, rope ladders, and grappling hooks to facilitate escapes. Useful potions, such as Truth Serum in a Bottle, Cloning Fluid in a Jug, and Antidote in a Bottle, are plentiful. Large ticket items include cardboard barrels containing armored robots and a teleportation storage drum. All proceeds support 826NYC, a nonprofit writing and tutoring program for NYC students ages six to eighteen, so buying anything here really does make you a hero.

•••••••••••••••••••••

Prevent scurvy before or after boarding the Waterfront Museum barge with plenty of Vitamin C from **Steve's Authentic Key Lime Pies** (204 Van Dyke Street, 718.858.5333). Each pie is made with fresh-squeezed Key limes, packing a tart wallop in the velvety filling. Individual or whole pies can be bought at the counter from friendly staff. An oasis in an industrial park in Red Hook, Steve's semi-successfully recreates the laid-back vibe of the Florida Keys outside the bakery with an adorable waterfall garden, picnic benches, and tables with unmatched chairs. It's bliss in a pie. I was "forced" to eat a second slice when my vegetarian friend Des realized that the pies contain gelatin. Woe is me.

WEEKSVILLE HERITAGE CENTER

Address: 1698–1708 Bergen Street

Phone: 718.756.5250

@, Directions: A or C to Utica Avenue; 3 or 4 to Crown
    Heights - Utica Avenue

Other details at: www.WeeksvilleSociety.org

Few things unnerve me more than the idea that an entire village can somehow disappear while remaining in plain sight. This is what happened to an African-American community in Brooklyn. Founded by James Weeks in 1838, the isolated, self-sufficient settlement attracted people fleeing violence against blacks in New York City as well as those escaping slavery in the South. Artisans, unskilled laborers, and professionals lived side-by-side. At its peak, Weeksville had its own school, orphanage, newspaper (Freedman's Torch Light), and home for the elderly. It also had the highest rate of property ownership among African-Americans in the country. The Great Depression, which hit people of color hardest, severely impacted the populations of Weeksville, and by the 1950s, many of the homes had fallen into disrepair. As newer roads and housing were built, the dilapidated remains of Weeksville's seven blocks "disappeared."

Uncovered when a local historian rented a plane and

from overhead noticed an oddly situated lane with four houses on it, today visitors can enter three fully restored homes capturing different eras of Weeksville's inspiring history. The only way to see what is left of the town is to take a tour, which is what I did one afternoon, starting with a double house that may have been occupied by the Pearson family in 1860. According to my guide, Rebecca Pearson was a schoolteacher and her husband Jacob a musician. They had one child. Their two-bedroom home (with just enough room for a bed in each of the bedrooms, as was the case with many homes in those times) has a carpeted living room and a mud room. The kitchen is outside.

The second house I visited is a two-story wood-frame house inhabited by the Johnsons in 1900, who resided there until 1927. While many women at the time took jobs as domestics outside of the community, Mrs. Johnson worked as a dressmaker and homemaker. Mr. Johnson was employed by a wagon company. The couple had nine children and two grandchildren. While the kitchen has no indoor plumbing, the mud room boasts a wood icebox. A copper boiler found during an archeological dig in the area was placed in the room to show how people washed clothes. The living room (which may have doubled as a bedroom) had gas lighting. My guide showed me a picture of Dr. Susan Smith-McKinney, the first African-American woman doctor in New York State, who lived in Weeksville. Two bedrooms are upstairs and include "dry sinks," in which a bucket of water had to be brought in to wash with. When restoring the home, workers found a trove of WWI-era tin soldiers in the attic.

A member of the Williams family, who occupied the third house on my tour, still lived in her family's home when Weeksville was "rediscovered" in 1968. Mr. Williams worked as a janitor and was a skilled carpenter who customized the elegant house. Mrs. Williams was a homemaker. They had four girls and one boy. With the assistance of one of the Williams' daughters, the building is restored to the way it appeared in 1930, during the Depression. As we chatted outside the house, the tour guide showed me the sun porch that Mr. Williams built. Nearby, a grindstone from the 1900s is still sharp enough that the Weeksville Society's groundskeeper uses it to sharpen his tools.

The kitchen is modern, with an electric stove and plumbing. A hot comb sits on the stove for the Williams women to straighten their hair. In the dining room, the polished hardwood floors glow. Custom French doors separate it from the living room and a beveled glass door hides a linen closet. A Victrola displayed near the telephone plays Marian Anderson and Paul Robeson recordings. Upstairs, the parents' bedroom is decorated with art deco furniture and the girls' bedroom has a built-in bookshelf.

The Weeksville Heritage Center provides a crucial look into an important community that was almost forgotten. In visiting the site, I felt that I had a unique opportunity to support cultural and historic preservation. At the same time, it served as a warning that poverty, discrimination, and unchecked development can destroy marginalized communities. I hope that others will see the wonderful community that existed at Weeksville and heed the warning before we "forget" other important places.

FLOYD BENNETT FIELD

Address: Jamaica Bay Gateway Park

Phone: 718.338.3799

@> Directions: 2 to Flatbush Avenue; then Q35 to the park
    entrance

Other details at: www.nps.gov/nr/travel/aviation/flo.htm

Floyd Bennett Field was the first commercial airport in
New York City. It opened its gates (literally—people
walked up to a gate on the fenced off field to board; suddenly it occurred to me where the term "boarding gate"
originated) in 1931, becoming the second busiest airport
in the nation within two years. By the time the Navy took
control of the site ten years later, Floyd Bennett Field had
ushered thousands of people to locales around the world.

I learned about the history of the airport in the Ryan
Visitor Center, which is housed in the former art
deco–style terminal. The building is not in good condition, but it still took little for me to imagine the hustle and
bustle of the good old days. An enthusiastic, retired Navy
veteran served as our tour guide. He pointed out the
rooms that served as the waiting area and cafeteria,
which today are used as classrooms. Unfortunately, many
of the luxurious finishes like marble countertops were
ripped out when the Navy acquired the site. I wandered
around in the lobby for a bit, looking at the displays on

the history of aviation while waiting for the tour of the upstairs to begin.

The second floor is a disaster area. My husband and I were shocked that visitors are allowed to go upstairs, even with a guide. Plaster and wiring hang down from the walls in the hallways and in the rooms that served as quarters for pilots to rest overnight before continuing long journeys at daybreak. (Flying at night was not an option in the 1930s.) Anyone who plans to explore the terminal should wear solid shoes.

We followed our guide up a maze of staircases. After climbing the final set of steep and narrow steps, we emerged in the control tower. The view of the four runways was incredible. Both original runways from 1931 are 100 feet wide. They meet in a T-shape, one runway 4,200 feet long and the other only 3,110 feet long. Two more runways were added in 1938, the year before the airport's commercial activities ceased. These are much longer, with one extending 4,000 feet and the other 5,500 feet long. Parked at the back of one of the runways was a white blimp.

"What's with the blimp?" I asked the guide.

"Oh, that? That's an unmarked police blimp," he replied. "You never saw it. Shhhh . . ."

On either side of the control tower are the airport's hangars. One former hangar complex is now used as a recreation center. While the battleship museum *The Intrepid* is under repair, the Concorde and a small plane are parked next to the recreation center, open for visits.

The other hangars house old aircraft, which are brought onto the runways at various times of the year for special events. Supposedly, the public is welcome to observe the restoration of twelve aircraft in Hangar B on Mondays, Wednesdays, and Saturdays, but when I went on a Saturday, my volunteer guide told me that the hangar is closed. He reported that it should be open in 2008 or 2009 when security clearance is granted.

Floyd Bennett Field also offers a small museum. Mostly the museum is dedicated to the airport's days under Navy supervision. Navy plaques and commemorative buttons consist of a good portion of the exhibit. However, a plaque noting that Willy Post landed the *Winnie Mae* on this site in 1933, breaking the previous record for an around-the-world flight. Post's travels took "only" 7 days, 18 hours, and 49 minutes that year. Sometimes I feel like I have to wait that long to use the lavatory when I'm on a long flight.

A tiny gift shop hocks books on aviation and World War II, stuffed lions, and other knickknacks. Standing in the gift shop nook, I thought about what it might have been like to buy a souvenir in that space when the airport was shiny and new.

ENRICO CARUSO MUSEUM OF AMERICA

Address: 1942 E. 19th Street
Phone: 718.368.3993
🏛️ Directions: Q to Avenue U
Other details at: www.EnricoCarusoMuseum.com
🍀 Appointments are required.

Forty years ago, Aldo Mancusi began collecting artifacts related to his favorite opera singer, Enrico Caruso. To honor his efforts to promote Caruso's work, the Italian government granted Mancusi the title of *Cavaliere Ufficiale*. ("It's like being knighted, but I can't pass the title down to my children when I die," he explained proudly.) Sitting in the museum in the second-story apartment of his two-family home in Brooklyn, I was amazed at what he's done.

Appointments are required to visit the museum. Mancusi gives visitors a two-hour lecture on the life of Caruso and opera in general while showing off the highlights of his collection and demonstrating various antique jukeboxes, phonographs, and music boxes. Visitors sit on chairs donated from opera singer Licia Albanese's personal box at the old Metropolitan Opera House. Although Mancusi threw in jokes about his wife and general business advice throughout the talk, I found it hard to focus on his words.

The museum is crammed from floor to rafters with Caruso paraphernalia and relics. A display case holds

Caruso's bling: a two-inch rectangular citron pendant and matching ring that he gave his first mistress, who took pity on his penniless son after Caruso died and passed it on to him. Caruso's costume from *Rigoletto* dresses a mannequin in a corner next to the case. Framed postcards from Caruso's world travels for his performances hang on the wall. The singer's pipe, shoes, fork and spoon, and cane are here, too. Caruso liked to doodle caricatures, and dozens are framed and hung. On the back of the door, a homemade poster-size family tree illustrates Caruso's bloodlines, complete with photos. Mancusi owns piles of one-hundred-year-old recordings. The crown jewel of the collection is Caruso's death mask—it's only one of three in the world.

Despite all the distractions, it was impossible to not pay attention when Mancusi played music. On a Berliner phonograph from 1895, a very scratchy recording of the popular Neapolitan song "Santa Lucia" filled my ears. (Pathetically, I recognized it from a Tom & Jerry cartoon when Tom sings the song while paddling in a pot under a crescent moon, but I digress.) A remarkably clear Neapolitan love song recorded by Caruso in 1910 was played next on a hand-wound, 1906 Victor machine, with translations provided by Mancusi. My eyes filled with tears as I listened, and I understood why Caruso is considered the greatest tenor ever.

After several false starts, Mancusi convinced the 1927 Mills Troubadour jukebox that he rebuilt to throw on the right tune. This is done by an internal revolving wheel that holds the records. Like Caruso's death mask, this is one of three of these machines known to exist. Next, a player piano with stained glass panels, housing an accordion and drum in the glassed-in compartment on the bottom, joyously filled the room with tunes before we walked over to the museum's back rooms.

A hodgepodge of items are on display in the bedroom. Licia Albanese's costume from *Madama Butterfly* graces one corner, and two costumes from other operas are displayed on mannequins diagonally across the way. A cherub and several structural elements from the old Met share space with a brick from the opera house in Venice. For no discernable reason, the room also stores several metal pieces of the Brooklyn Bridge.

"What's with the bridge?" I asked Mancusi.

"Oh, this is also my museum on the Brooklyn Bridge," the man of many interests answered affably.

We move into the dining room. In any other place, this room would be a museum in and of itself. Phonographs that played cylinders of recorded sound fill the room, including a Thomas Edison Standard Cylinder Phonograph painted with roses in the speaker. Mancusi demonstrated a cylinder with five instruments and a human voice recorded in 1900. He also has an Edison tin foil recorder from 1878 and a Dictaphone. A music box from 1870 entertained upper-middle-class folks with ten different opera selections. Even better, the 1895 Mira music box offered refined listeners different metal discs of music, not unlike CDs, albeit a bit tinnier. Mancusi fooled me by playing an accordion that runs on paper players that produce the tunes automatically.

My museum visit came to a close in the custom built Piccolo Teatro Enrico Caruso. Mancusi furnished the theater with seats from the former Loews Theater on 46th Street and Utrecht Avenue, so I watched clips from various documentaries on Caruso (and a few shows about the museum and Mancusi) in comfort. On my way out, I noticed that the kitchen does double duty as a Puccini room and small gift shop. Of course, it sells opera books and CDs.

Photos courtesy of Roger Chi

CONEY ISLAND MUSEUM

Address: 1208 Surf Avenue

Phone: 718.372.5159

Directions: D, F, N, or Q to Coney Island

Other details at: www.ConeyIsland.com/museum.shtml

The labels on each rickety stairstep leading up to the Coney Island Museum pay homage to each unnatural wonder of the world that Coney Island boasted at some point in its storied history as the playground of New Yorkers. Upstairs, when I forked over a crisp dollar bill to cover my 99-cent admission, the woman behind the counter told me to keep my penny change handy for the penny movie, which she warned shows a graphic depiction of the electrocution of the circus elephant Topsy. I was appropriately horrified, but also intrigued.

The museum room is a mostly explanation-free collection of items and photographs from Coney Island's days of glory presented in no particular order that I could discern. There's a stage at the front of the room and folding chairs set up theater style for performances and events. Most of the items in the museum are grouped around the perimeter wall.

The first artifacts I encountered were from the Mermaid Parade, which celebrated its twenty-fifth year in 2007. The parade is held on the Saturday following the vernal equinox to welcome the official start of summer. Generally, marchers adorn themselves in sea-themed costumes, and the mermaids are joined by all sorts of colorful water-based friends. The museum wall is covered by posters advertising the Mermaid Parade over the last two and a half decades. A child-sized, gold spray-painted Model-T with silver, green, and blue glitter accents sits next to the entrance to the museum room, under the posters. Nearby are a six-foot-tall seashell that opened the twenty-fifth annual parade and a kid's wagon with an elaborately painted seascape, including plastic toy fish glued on for a 3-D effect.

On the other side of the stage is a display dedicated to Lilly's World in Wax, a mainstay of Coney Island from 1923–1981. Artifacts from the wax museum include a roll of entrance tickets, a finger tip, a hand, and a bald head with beady glass eyes and a mustache. Photos of Lilly outside her business and a sign discussing the history of wax museums makes me wish I had firsthand experience with Brooklyn's precursor to Madame Toussauds in person.

Underneath antique signs advertising embroidered hats, I gazed into a display case with photographs of the Dreamland Social Club from 1923 and 1924. Other pictures exhibited along with these group shots are individual portraits of "Sealo the Seal Boy," a guy with chipmunk cheeks, and a man decked out in a captain's hat holding two shrunken heads. No notes explain who the people in these photos are, although I assumed the last three subjects worked at the sideshows that used to entice thousands of curiosity seekers to part with their hard-earned cash.

Next, I viewed a small exhibit with souvenirs of all sorts. Spoons, ashtrays, shell-encrusted jewelry boxes, and other junk spanning the decades are not so different from what is sold in crap shops on Surf Avenue today. Old postcards depict people whooping it up. Menus and tickets dated 1913 from Stauch's dance hall and restaurant provide a glimpse into how much entertainment cost almost one hundred years ago.

In its heyday, Coney Island had something for everyone. Wood stilts are propped against the wall next to a slot machine from the time when Atlantic City was not the only boardwalk that allowed gambling. Kids of all ages could get the rides of their lives on everything from the museum's 1890 wooden carousel horse with most of its paint chipped off to the faded yellow-and-blue metal rocket ship ride that seats two tots, each provided with a handy, mounted swivel gun. Bumper cars of various sizes fill the middle of the room. No less dangerous, two wicker "rolling chairs"—sort of like rickshaws, but pushed from behind—with striped cushions circa 1905 provided me with insight into what transportation was available to those who tired of strolling on the boardwalk.

If rides didn't do it for people, there were always games to be played. The museum displays a number of old amusements, many of which are still popular at carnivals today. Decades ago, I could discover my love personality type by squeezing the metal prongs on the wooden "Love Meter." (Would I register as bashful, jealous, flirtatious, cold, or lovable?) My luck could be tested by the games of chance on clacking yellow-and-red painted wooden wheels of chance, each slot a number. If I was really fortunate, my sweetheart could demonstrate his strength to the world at large by swinging the now rotted hammer and hitting the target on the strong-man machine.

After observing the tools of fun used in yesteryear, and reading stories about Luna Park, Dreamland, Steeplechase Park, and Sea Lion Park, the amusement emporiums that proffered them, I came across the museum's Mutoscope. After inserting my penny, sticking my face into the goggles on the machine, and cranking the handle, the flip cards began turning quickly, showing me in smoking, sad detail the story of Thomas Edison's electrocution of Topsy the Elephant. The placard on the museum wall explains that, after years of abuse by her cruel caretaker at Luna Park, Topsy was prompted to (justifiably, in my mind) kill him after he fed her a lit cigarette. In turn, Topsy was sentenced to death by electrocution, and in memoriam to the pachyderm, the Mutoscope film shows poor Topsy's demise.

While Topsy's story is a downer, the show must go on, and Coney Island is about nothing if not fun. A signless niche behind the Mutoscope displays an awesome collection of thermoses, coolers, and kegs, which appear to my untrained eye to be from the 1940s-1960s. A display case holds a 1940s-style bathing suit tank top and girl's swim cap bedecked with a bow on top. Tickets to different bath-houses fill the case as well. Beside a stack of canvas beach chairs, two chairs are set beneath an umbrella, modeling a day of sand and sun from some decades ago.

On the way out, I stopped in front of the five funhouse mirrors and chuckled at my distorted reflection. (No, I'm not *really* that short and fat, I swear!) The nice little gift shop purveys both reproduction and antique postcards, books, T-shirts, and other appropriate Coney Island souvenirs.

Grab a hot dog or fried clams from **Nathan's Famous** (1310 Surf Avenue, 718.946.2022) and eat like New Yorkers did back in 1916. According to legend, the infamous Nathan's hot dog eating contest began that year when four European immigrants settled a bet about who was more patriotic by setting out to eat the most hot dogs. Chow down on your dog while viewing the more recent history of the Nathan's Hot Dog Eating Contest around the corner on Stillwell Avenue, where the Nathan's Wall of Fame honors the men and women with elastic stomachs. Atop a mural depicting the hot dog eating stars of today (I immediately recognized Takeru "The Tsunami" Kobayashi, Sonya "The Black Widow" Thomas, Eric "Badlands" Booker, and Ed "Cookie" Jarvis), a digital clock counts down the days, hours, minutes, and seconds to the next July 4th competition. Under the motto "They Came. They Ate. They Conquered. All in 12 Minutes" is a list of champions dating back to 1984. Compare 2007's winner Joey Chestnut (66 hot dogs) to 1984's champ Birgit Feldon (9.5) to see just how far we've advanced in the past few decades.

Courtesy of Roger Chi

HARBOR DEFENSE MUSEUM

Address: US Army Garrison Fort Hamilton, 230 Sheridan Loop
Phone: 718.630.4349
> Directions: R to 95th Street
Other details at: www.HarborDefenseMuseum.com
Advance notice required.

I sauntered over to the Harbor Defense Museum, clueless about its location on an active army base. (Who knew there were army outposts in Brooklyn?) Thus I learned that it is important to call ahead to let the museum staff know that you are coming, so they can alert the garrison's visitor center to expect you. Fortunately, someone answered the phone at the museum when I called while standing outside the visitor center. They then called the visitor center to approve my visit, and only then was I allowed in.

While walking to the museum, which is housed inside the brick walls of Fort Hamilton's virtually unaltered 1825 caponier (a small building behind the main fort, situated in its dry moat and constructed for rear defense), I passed by many retired tanks, cannons, and other large weapons. All were nicely explained by signs, noting each piece's dates of use and purpose, which pleased me immensely. I walked through the heavy arched wooden door of the museum with high hopes.

Inside, small groups of senior citizens wandered around with volunteer staff. As I studied a display case with replica Hessian, Scottish, and British uniforms from the Revolutionary War era, an elderly man approached me.

"I'm Irwin, and I participated in the invasion of Sicily during World War II," he informed me. "Is anyone showing you around?"

I shook my head, and he said he would be my guide. Irwin explained the history of the fort. Before it was fortified, the first battle of the post-Declaration of Independence Revolutionary War took place on the site of what was to become Fort Hamilton when a small battery of Americans fired upon a British ship sent to suppress the revolt. The resulting Battle of Brooklyn did not end well for the rebels.

Mainly, Irwin's tour involved mocking early Americans, noting that the Continental Army at first consisted of illiterate farmers, bums, and drunks. "The British couldn't understand how these rednecks managed to kill any of their soldiers," he confided as he showed me drawings and maps documenting battles from the Revolutionary War. Regarding the subsequent War of 1812, Irwin asked me, "Everyone hears about how the British provoked the War of 1812 through conscription, but did you know that the American yahoos who lived on the border of Canada irritated British loyalists by getting drunk, crossing into their territory, and raising hell?" I did not, but was entertained to learn this. A mannequin dressed in an antique military uniform crouched in a defensive position at a window, and Irwin patted its shoulder as we passed.

The Harbor Defense Museum is full of antique weapons. Irwin walked me past several cannon models and explained innovations in cannon technology and ammunition. He showed me a ten-inch mortar shell with handles that soldiers had to fill with gunpowder before loading and firing. A small cannon, its barrel broken and smashed, illustrates how new technology rendered older cannons useless and even smashed through fortifications, requiring continually upgraded and improved weapons for defense. The most interesting cannon on display is an 1844 Flank Howitzer mounted on a half circle track that could be rotated for better aim. Positioned toward land, the weapon was designed to obliterate enemy forces that approached from behind the fort.

After thirty minutes, I'd seen guns, missiles, and weapons from the 1770s through World War II, and Irwin hustled me to the door. Before leaving Ft. Hamilton's gate, I stopped at a rock in front of the garrison's legal building with a plaque on it from the Daughters of the Confederacy noting that the traitor (my description, of course) Robert E. Lee served at Ft. Hamilton from 1841–1846. At the gate leading back into civilian territory, I admired the largest smoothbore, muzzle-loading coastal defense gun ever built in the United States. It's quite a country that I live in.

In quiet, leafy **John Paul Jones Park** (bounded by Shore Road, Fourth Avenue, 101st Street, and Fort Hamilton Parkway), a ginormous black cannon faces the Verrazano Bridge, warning Staten Islanders to keep to their side of the Narrows or else. A row of nine beach-ball-sized cannon balls sits in front of the cannon, and four piles of five balls each are stacked behind it. The twenty-inch bore, 1864 Parrott cannon originally stood in Fort Pitt, Pennsylvania, and was placed in the park in 1900 as a Civil War memorial. A boulder situated deeper in the five-acre park bears a plaque from 1916, "To commemorate the first resistance made to British arms in New York State, August 1776." Near the back of "Cannon Ball Park" is a monument to Giovanni da Verrazzano, the first European to sail through the Narrows, and Brooklynite John LaCorte, who tirelessly promoted Italian achievements before his death in 1991. Thanks to LaCorte's advocacy, Columbus Day is a national holiday and the forgotten explorer da Verrazzano became the namesake of a bridge to Staten Island.

Courtesy of S. Pollack

STATEN

ISLAND

STATEN ISLAND MUSEUM

Address: 75 Stuyvesant Place

Phone: 718.727.1135

Directions: Staten Island Ferry to Staten Island

Other details at: www.StatenIslandMuseum.org

Like everyone, I sometimes just want to see dead stuffed things or insects pinned to boards. Most people indulge their bloodlust by heading over to the enormous, crowded Museum of Natural History. Those who prefer to spend time communing with deceased critters in a more intimate setting, however, can visit the Staten Island Museum.

Founded in 1881 as the Natural Science Association of Staten Island, this four-gallery museum has bugs, taxidermied animals, geological displays, "curious objects," and information on the wonders of the Staten Island Ferry, which is just a short walk away. Visitors can enjoy the Wall of Insects, containing butterflies, beetles, moths, cicadas, and an exceptionally gross, pallid stick insect, before even approaching the admissions desk. The elderly man at the desk waited patiently for me while I studied the impaled six-legged critters and made faces.

The highlight of the museum is the Hall of Natural Science. This large room contains nine more glass boxes of insects mounted on the wall, as well as a large collection of preserved dead animals. The Victorian shadow box in the room is 120 years old and crammed with furry and feathered friends. Butterflies and moths flit about as a mink perpetually clamps its teeth into the neck of a chicken, a squirrel jaws a fake acorn, and bats hang upside down while a perturbed-looking owl glares at anyone who gazes upon the scene. People of the Victorian age, I was informed by the sign on the box, loved elaborate scenes like this one.

The Hall of Science also has a glass display case with a completely random assortment of specimens in formaldehyde. Some jars hold more than one critter of the same species; others are slightly too small for the one unfortunate creature that is stuffed inside it. I marveled at preserved animals ranging from salamanders to a blue grosbeak nestling to long-finned squid eggs to morel mushrooms.

Along the wall behind the case of formaldehyde jars is the Display of Strange Things. This is my favorite part of the museum. A helpful sign explains that any museum that has operated for more than one hundred years is destined to wind up with specimens that defy classification. The Staten Island Museum's collection of oddities includes both the truly amazing and the utterly mundane. The best of the best are a solid hairball from a cow's stomach, a four-legged chicken, "a tusk from the wild boar which I shot in Louisiana swamps, but not until he had killed my dog," and the rind of a four-pound lemon. Inexplicably included in this collection is a matchbox from the 1940s full of rabbit turds.

The remainder of the Hall of Science contains rocks and more stuffed animals. After a cursory look at the unexciting Staten Island Ferry historical collection, I headed upstairs. The second-floor gallery contains rotating art exhibits, as well as even more bugs on display from the museum's 500,000-strong collection. There is also a small hallway containing a display case with plates and glassware from the 1700s to modern times.

Before leaving the museum, it is worth a stop at the gift shop counter for cheesy souvenirs. From books about Staten Island to bugs in pendants, mood rings, lighthouse sculptures, and Golden Guides to nature (two titles: *Bats of the World* and *Spiders and Their Kind*), the tiny shop leaves no stone unturned.

Between the ferry terminal and the Staten Island Museum lies the Richmond County Bank Ballpark, home to the Staten Island Yankees. Visible through the black wrought iron fence is the **Professional Baseball Scouting Hall of Fame**. Wander over and take a gander at the plaques paying tribute to seven great baseball scouts.

OUR LADY OF MT. CARMEL SHRINE

Address: 36 Amity Street

Phone: none

✆→ Directions: Staten Island Ferry, then S81 bus to Hylan Boulevard

Other Details at: www.MountCarmelSociety.com

A dead-end street in a residential neighborhood harbors Our Lady of Mt. Carmel Shrine, one of the greatest religious treasures in New York City. The shrine is open 24 hours a day next to Mt. Carmel Hall, a rickety white wooden structure that looks like it will collapse in the next strong wind. Enter the site through a chainlink fence with two signs. The first is a stone tablet announcing Our Lady of Mt. Carmel, spelled out in pebbles and stones stuck into the tablet's surface. More formally, a large wooden sign announces that the shrine is a Historic Landmark site.

Originally built in the 1930s by an Italian immigrant, Vito Luis Russell, the shrine has expanded over the years and been carefully maintained by the Our Lady of Mt. Carmel Society. The shrine is a concrete grotto, decorated with glass, marbles, plastic, seashells, and thousands of stones and pebbles sunk into its elaborate form. Some of the niches for statues, candles, or other objects have light bulbs in them; others are glassed over to protect their contents.

Courtesy of Scott Pollack

The grotto is similar to a cathedral, with a main alter and chapels flanking it. Obviously, the main altar is the most elaborate part of the shrine. A statue of Mary and baby Jesus rests in a niche at the center near a yellow glass cross embedded in concrete. The two figures have gold filigree crowns upon their heads, and multiple rosaries and medallions are draped over them. They are surrounded by dozens of personal pictures and mementos of loved ones in need of divine intervention, or prayers for those who have already departed. Precious Moments figurines, crosses, and a picture of New York City Mayor Michael Bloomberg visiting the shrine add to the surreal effect.

The flanking arms of the shrine have stained glass in some parts, and a large bell hangs in a bell tower on the arm to the right of the main altar. Separate from the main grotto structure is a monument reading, "Our Lady of Mount Carmel, God Bless All," written with stones set in the concrete. A stone-covered concrete fountain sits in the center of it all. The water was not running during my visit. Contemplate the miraculous structure from one of the benches on the grounds.

Every July, a feast is held on the grounds. The pavilion behind the grotto contains a full-service bar, and food and carnival games are enjoyed by all ages. There is no gift shop.

GARIBALDI MEUCCI MUSEUM

Address: 420 Tompkins Avenue

Phone: 718.442.1608

Directions: Staten Island Ferry, then S78 or S52 to the corner of Tompkins and Chestnut Avenues

Other details at: www.GaribaldiMeucciMuseum.org

Italians insist that their fellow countryman Antonio Meucci invented the telephone and that Alexander Graham Bell stole his invention. Until my visit to the Garibaldi Meucci Museum, I toed the conventional line, believing the song from "Bye Bye Birdie" and crediting the Scotsman with creating the technology that I abused as a chatty teenager.

Born and trained in Florence, Meucci came to the United States from Cuba in 1850, where he worked at creating and implementing elaborate stage sets at the opera house. While in Cuba, the brilliant Meucci also invented a water purification filter and numerous other devices, including a "talking telegraph." At his delightful white wooden cottage in Staten Island, Meucci continued to innovate, inventing a smokeless candle. After Gen. Giuseppe Garibaldi fled Italy later that year, he stayed with the Meucci family and helped them make candles in the specially designed backyard furnace that remains behind the house. Garibaldi eventually returned to Italy, where he successfully reunited the country. He lived out his remaining days in peace on the island of Sardina. Unfortunately, unlike his friend, Meucci did not benefit from his hard work over the years. His greatest invention was stolen, and despite selling many others, he struggled to make ends meet until he died in poverty.

The Garibaldi Meucci Museum pays equal tribute to both of these great Italian men. A guide first played a video about the men for me, then escorted me through the house on a personal tour. The ground floor has a display case with the Gen. Garibaldi's clothes, eyeglasses, revolver, field whistle, tobacco pipe, and a swatch of hair in one room. The room also provides information about Garibaldi's campaign to unite Italy. Turns out that Lincoln was so impressed with Garibaldi's work that he asked him to head the U.S. Army. Garibaldi agreed to do so under two conditions: first, that all slaves be freed; second, that he be allowed to work with no interference. At the time, those requests were deemed unacceptable, so off Garibaldi went to Italy to fulfill his destiny to make the nation a great center of food and fashion.

The other gallery on the ground floor is dedicated to Meucci. On display are Meucci's death mask, an elaborate chair hand carved by the inventor, a piano he built, and most important, copies of models of his telephone invention. He had sent the models to the American District Telegraph Company, where a young Alexander Graham Bell was employed. Once Meucci's patent expired, the

company claimed they "lost" the Meucci's prototypes, and Graham Bell patented the work for himself.

Upstairs, I was treated to the recreated bedroom that Garibaldi used while living here. The General's red embroidered shirt is laid out on the bed with his hat and tobacco pouch, and his walking stick is propped up at the foot of the bed. The room also has the shaving mirror and a chair that he used, as well as weapons from the era. A library down the hall contains books on Italian culture and is open to the public.

The museum sports a gift hutch that sells the video on Meucci and Garibaldi shown to visitors upon arrival. It also offers various Italian paraphernalia, such as mini flags and key chains.

The **Castleton Hill Moravian Church Labyrinth Walk** (1657 Victory Boulevard, 718.442.5215) is not conveniently located near anything unless you are on your way to the Staten Island Mall. However, given the dearth of labyrinths in New York City, labyrinth lovers will find it is worth hopping on a bus to quickly check out. I expected something like a huge corn maze, and was initially disappointed when I arrived at the church to see that the labyrinth is imprinted in the brickwork in the church courtyard. Paper guides to walking the tiny labyrinth and seeking spiritual solace are available outside. Indoors, the church offers CDs and finger labyrinths. The maze is next to the church preschool playground, so try to avoid visiting when the children are likely to be using it.

NOBLE MARITIME COLLECTION

Address: Snug Harbor Cultural Center, 1000 Richmond Terrace, Building D
Phone: 718.447.6490
@, Directions: Staten Island Ferry, then S40 to the front gate of Snug Harbor Cultural Center
Other details at: www.NobleMaritime.org

Snug Harbor opened in the 1830s as a retirement home for sailors. The property quickly expanded to a large campus with multiple dormitories, a hospital, and other facilities. As modern social programs left fewer retired sailors destitute, the demand for group housing declined. The facility closed in the 1970s, leaving behind five Greek revival-style buildings, one of which now houses the Noble Maritime Collection.

Extensive restoration work on the building revealed patterned wood floors and stained glass windows in the museum, which is named in honor of John A. Noble. Noble was the son of the artist John "Wichita Bill" Noble, who became famous in the first part of the twentieth century for his luminescent paintings. (Not many of these exist today, the museum staff member confessed to me, because it is suspected that the senior Noble created his shimmery light effects by mixing butter with his paint. Needless to say, this does not make for lasting work.) John

A. fell in love with New York Harbor, worked on schooners, and spent his artistic career painting "maritime endeavors." Two galleries in the museum exhibit paintings by Wichita Bill and John A Noble.

After quitting the schooner industry, John A. wanted to remain in New York Harbor as he painted. He built a boat from scrap material he scavenged from a ship graveyard to use for his studio. The body of the boat is the teak saloon of a European yacht, but elements of tugboat and other ship styles make it unique. The boat was docked in New York Harbor until he died in 1983. It was taken apart and piece by piece rebuilt at the Noble Collection, where it was recreated to look as it did in 1954 when Noble was featured in *National Geographic*. A staff member took me on the boat. The tiny quarters hold a wood-burning stove, a pantry, and a bunk that John could rest on during breaks from painting, all surrounded by dark brown wood polished to a glow. John's easel is set up as though he'll emerge any second from the seafoam-green bathroom nook at the back of the ship and start painting again.

The other highlights of the collection are the two restored rooms from the building's turn-of-the-century retirement home days. The Writing Room, on the first floor, is set with historic furnishings, including a wood-and-wicker wheelchair. On the ceiling, a mural created the sensation that I was standing under a trellis in a garden. The room also displays antique postcards of the Snug Harbor grounds, reprinted drawings of the facility that appeared in *Harper's Magazine* in the 1860s and 1870s, and portraits of residents from 1907 to 1908.

I strolled up the blond wood grand staircase to the second floor to see the recreated dorm room from 1900. Two metal beds facing toe-to-toe line the right wall of the long, narrow rectangular room. Small shelves holding grooming products are attached above the beds. A stall with a curtain, presumably for changing in private, occupies the far left corner. Leaning against the left wall is a dresser with wooden slabs jutting out from the sides serving as writing tables. A chair and a rocking chair complete the furnishings. Although seemingly spartan, the room was luxurious compared to the conditions that the weary sailors suffered on their ships.

The remainder of the second floor holds the Collection's library, a meeting room, and several classrooms for school children. The guy working at the museum encouraged me to go into those rooms, and many of them had naval tools for the kids to handle. The Soul of a Sail classroom even had a mural in a nook that creates the illusion of being below deck in a listing wooden ship on a wave. I literally felt seasick standing near it.

The best way to appreciate the beautiful condition the building is in today is to stop into the Noble Crew Exhibit room. The volunteers who refurbished the property purposely left this room untouched. As I looked at chunks of plastic missing from light green walls and the holes in the wood frame of the ceiling, I was extra grateful for the amazing work that had gone into making Building D a literal showroom. John A. Santore, a firefighter who spear-headed the restoration project until he was killed at the World Trade Center on 9/11, is honored in this touching space.

In the gift shop, I scooped up two copies of a children's book written especially for the Noble Maritime Collection about a pirate who learns how to behave appropriately in a museum. Other items for purchase include the T-shirts, Noble art prints, model ships, mugs, and postcards.

INDEX BY CATEGORY

Art and Architecture
5 Pointz (Q), 156
14th Street A,C,E Subway Station (M), 56
258th Field Artillery Armory (BRX), 135
Cathedral of St. John the Divine (M), 101
Corning Gallery at Steuben Glass (M), 75
Dia Center for the Arts: The New York Earth Room and The Broken Kilometer (M), 44
Galeria De La Vega (M), 50
Hall of Fame for Great Americans (BRX), 136
Herbert and Eileen Bernard Museum of Judaica at Temple Emanu-El (M), 83
Highway living (M), 116
The Living Museum at Creedmoor Psychiatric Center (Q), 172
Malcolm Shabazz Mosque (M), 107
Museum of American Illustration (M), 80
Museum of Art and Origins (M), 110
Museum of Comic and Cartoon Art (M), 46
National Museum of Catholic Art & History/Our Lady of Mt. Carmel Church (M), 91
Nicholas Roerich Museum (M), 98
Nobel Maritime Collection (SI), 233
Prison Ship Martyrs Monument (BRK), 194

Queens Museum of Art (Q), 165
SKSK (BRK), 191
Skyscraper Museum (M), 21
Socrates Sculpture Park (Q), 153
Ukrainian Museum (M), 48
United Nations Sculpture Garden (M), 70

Eating
Albert's Mofongo House, 126
Amy Ruth's (M), 107
Astoria bakeries and food mini-tour (Q), 152
Bohemian Hall and Beer Garden (Q), 155
Economy Candy (M), 40
Eisenberg's Sandwich Shop (M), 61
El Malécon (M), 116
Fraunces Tavern Museum (M), 25
Hungarian Pastry Shop (M), 107
Jeremy's Ale House (M), 36
Little Lad's Basket (M), 34
Loeser's Kosher Delicatessen (BRX), 131
Nathan's Famous (BRK), 216
Pickles—Pickle Guys and Guss' (M), 40
Rice to Riches (M), 43
Steve's Authentic Key Lime Pies (BRK), 199
Yonah Schimmel's Knishery (M), 40

Ethnic
Albert's Mofongo House, 126
Astoria bakeries and food mini-tour (Q), 152

Bohemian Hall and Beer Garden (Q), 155

El Malécon (M), 116

Garibaldi Meucci Museum (SI), 229

Herbert and Eileen Bernard Museum of Judaica at Temple Emanu-El (M), 83

Hungarian Pastry Shop (M), 107

Judaica Museum of the Hebrew Home for the Aged (BRX), 129

Museum of Art and Origins (M), 110

National Museum of Catholic Art & History/Our Lady of Mt. Carmel Church (M), 91

Nicholas Roerich Museum (M), 98

Ukrainian Museum (M), 48

Weeksville Heritage Center (BRK), 200

Yonah Schimmel's Knishery (M), 40

Factory Tour

Brooklyn Brewery Tour (BRK), 189

Steinway & Sons Piano Factory Tour (Q), 149

Fort

Harbor Defense Museum (BRK), 217

Maritime Industry Museum at SUNY Maritime College (BRX), 142

Hall of Fame

Ertegun Jazz Hall of Fame (M), 97

Hall of Fame for Great Americans (BRX), 136

Masonic Hall and Chancellor Robert R. Livingston Masonic Library and Museum of Grand Lodge (M), 62

Nathan's Famous Hot Dog Eating Wall of Fame (BRK), 216

National Track and Field Hall of Fame (M), 113

Professional Baseball Scouting Hall of Fame (SI), 225

Historic

Aqueduct Walk (BRX), 138

Archeological dig sites (M), 28

Berlin Wall (M), 71

Dyckman Farmhouse Museum (M), 121

Edgar Allan Poe Cottage (BRX), 132

Floyd Bennett Field (BRK), 204

Ft. Washington, Site of (M), 116

Fraunces Tavern Museum (M), 25

Garibaldi Meucci Museum (SI), 229

Inwood Hill Park (M), 124

Mt. Vernon Hotel Museum & Garden (M), 76

Queens County Farm Museum (Q), 176

Theodore Roosevelt's Birthplace (M), 59

Trinity Cemetery and Mausoleum (M), 108

Weeksville Heritage Center (BRK), 200

Home-based

Enrico Caruso Museum of America (BRK), 207

Louis Armstrong House (Q), 158

Lower East Side Troll Museum (M), 37

Museum of Art and Origins (M), 110

Waterfront Museum (BRK), 196

Libraries

Horticultural Society of New York (M), 69

Masonic Hall and Chancellor Robert R. Livingston Masonic Library and Museum of Grand Lodge (M), 62

New York Academy of Medicine Library (M), 86

Money

American Numismatic Society/New York Federal Reserve Bank (M), 32

Museum of American Finance (M), 35

Music

Enrico Caruso Museum of America (BRK), 207
Ertegun Jazz Hall of Fame (M), 97
Louis Armstrong House (Q), 158
Steinway & Sons Piano Factory Tour (Q), 149

Nautical

Forbes Galleries (M), 51
Maritime Industry Museum at SUNY Maritime College (BRX), 142
Nobel Maritime Collection (SI), 233
Staten Island Museum (SI), 223
Waterfront Museum (BRK), 196

New York City–related

Aqueduct Walk (BRX), 138
Archeological dig sites (M), 28
City Reliquary (BRK), 183
Coney Island Museum (BRK), 211
Fraunces Tavern Museum (M), 25
Museum of the City of New York (M), 88
National Museum of Catholic Art & History/Our Lady of Mt. Carmel Church (M), 91
New York City Fire Museum (M), 41
New York City Police Museum (M), 29
New York City Transit Museum (BRK), 192
Poppenhusen Institute (Q), 169
Queens Museum of Art (Q), 176
Weeksville Heritage Center (BRK), 200

Oddities

Berlin Wall (M), 71
Castleton Hill Moravian Church Labyrinth Walk (SI), 232
Masonic Hall and Chancellor Robert R. Livingston Masonic Library and Museum of Grand Lodge (M), 62

New York Academy of Medicine Library (M), 86
Obscura Antiques (M), 50
Staten Island Museum (SI), 223
Waterfall Walkway (M), 71

Outdoor/Nature

Castleton Hill Moravian Church Labyrinth Walk (SI), 232
Charles A. Dana Discovery Center (M), 90
Dyckman Farmhouse Museum (M), 121
Ft. Washington, Site of (M), 116
Horticultural Society of New York (M), 69
Inwood Hill Park (M), 124
John Paul Jones Park (BRK), 220
Mini George Washington Bridge playground (M), 115
Mt. Vernon Hotel Museum & Garden (M), 76
Prison Ship Martyrs Monument (BRK), 194
Queens County Farm Museum (Q), 176
Socrates Sculpture Park (Q), 153
Staten Island Museum (SI), 223
Trinity Cemetery and Mausoleum (M), 108
United Nations Sculpture Garden (M), 70
Waterfall Walkway (M), 71

Religious/Spiritual

Castleton Hill Moravian Church Labyrinth Walk (SI), 232
Cathedral of St. John the Divine (M), 101
Chapel of Sacred Mirrors (M), 67
El Indio Amazonico (Q), 164

Herbert & Eileen Bernard Museum of Judaica at Temple Emanu-El (M), 83
Judaica Museum of the Hebrew Home for the Aged (BRX), 129
Malcolm Shabazz Mosque (M), 107
Masonic Hall and Chancellor Robert R. Livingston Masonic Library and Museum of Grand Lodge (M), 62
National Museum of Catholic Art & History/Our Lady of Mt. Carmel Church (M), 91
Nicholas Roerich Museum (M), 98
Original Products (BRX), 135
Our Lady of Lourdes Grotto at St. Lucy's Church (BRX), 139
Our Lady of Mt. Carmel Shrine (SI), 226
Shrine Church of Our Lady of Mt. Carmel (BRK), 187
St. Frances Cabrini Shrine (M), 117

Science and Technology
Garibaldi Meucci Museum (SI), 229
New York Academy of Medicine Library (M), 86
Staten Island Museum (SI), 223

Shrine
Fraunces Tavern Museum (M), 25
National Museum of Catholic Art & History/Our Lady of Mt. Carmel Church (M), 91
Our Lady of Lourdes Grotto at St. Lucy's Church (BRX), 139
Our Lady of Mt. Carmel Shrine (SI), 226
Shrine Church of Our Lady of Mt. Carmel (BRK), 187
St. Frances Cabrini Shrine (M), 117

Shopping
Brooklyn Superhero Supply Co. (BRK), 199

Economy Candy (M), 40
El Indio Amazonico (Q), 164
Galeria De La Vega (M), 50
Harlem Market (M), 107
Jumel Terrace Books (M), 112
Obscura Antiques (M), 50
Original Products (BRX), 135
Scavengers of Inwood (M), 123
SKSK (BRK), 191
Steve's Authentic Key Lime Pies (BRK), 199
Tender Buttons (M), 79

Sports
Museum of the City of New York (M), 88
National Track & Field Hall of Fame (M), 113
Professional Baseball Scouting Hall of Fame (SI), 225

Store-based
Corning Gallery at Steuben Glass (M), 75
Tourneau Gallery of Time and Oris Exhibit Hall (M), 72

Toys
Forbes Galleries (M), 51
Lower East Side Troll Museum (M), 37
Museum of the City of New York (M), 88

World's Largest/Tallest . . .
258th Field Artillery Armory (BRX), 135
Cathedral of St. John the Divine (M), 101
Herbert & Eileen Bernard Museum of Judaica at Temple Emanu-El (M), 83
Prison Ship Martyrs Monument (BRK), 194
Queens Museum of Art (Q), 165